HIGH INSPIRATION
mountains, running and creativity

 little peak press

This book is dedicated to my Dad.

High Inspiration – Heather Dawe

First published in 2019 by Little Peak Press

www.littlepeak.co.uk

This book is a work of non-fiction based on the life, experiences and recollections of Heather Dawe. In some limited cases the names of people, place, dates and sequences or the detail of events have been changed solely to protect the privacy of others. The author has stated to the publishers that, except in such minor respects not affecting the substantial accuracy of the work, the contents of the book are true.

Edited by Jo Allen

All illustrations by Heather Dawe

Design and Production by Rhiannon Hughes,
www.theyorkshirewordwright.co.uk

A CIP catalogue record for this book is available from the British Library.

ISBN: 978-1-9160812-0-8

Printed and bound in Wales by Cambrian Printers.

CONTENTS

Mont Blanc Massif

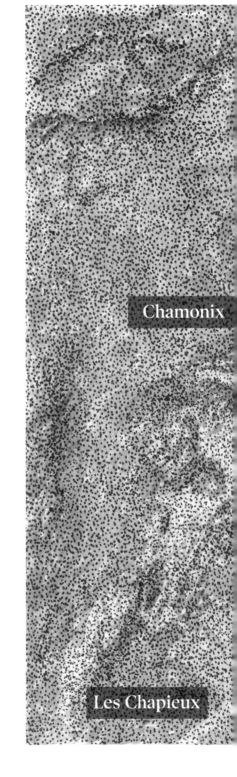

Chamonix

Les Chapieux

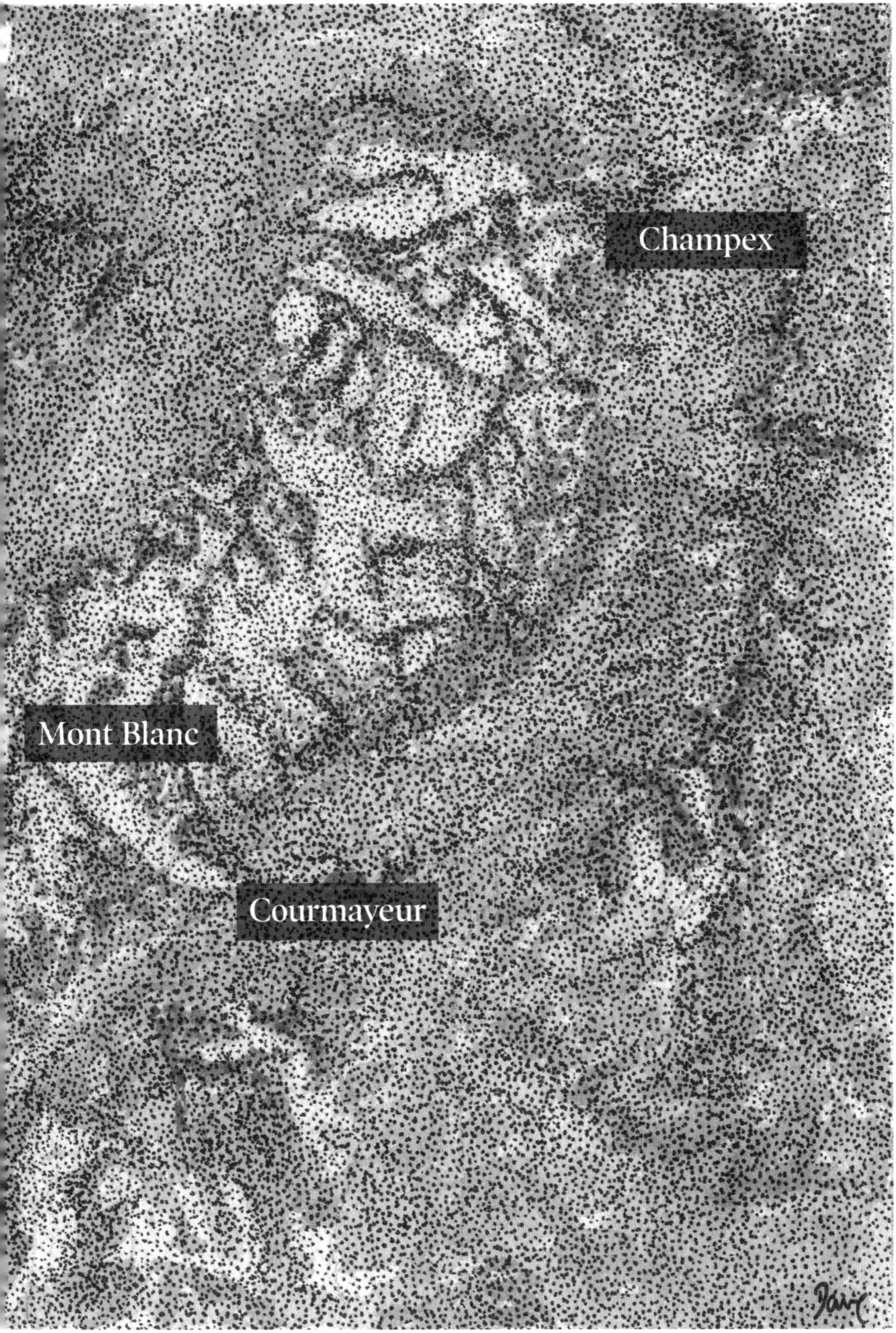
Champex
Mont Blanc
Courmayeur

'As far as Mont Blanc is concerned: well, I have always regarded it as a sort of ancestor that has taught me valuable lessons. Sometimes it punished me, but it has never really been too harsh with me. I return assiduously to its valleys and ridges, in the same spirit with which one returns to one's own father – to converse with him with all the affection and all the memories a son could wish for.'

Walter Bonatti, *The Mountains of My Life*

'Those that do not love them don't go up, and those who do can never have enough of it. It is an appetite that grows in feeding. Like drink and passion, it intensifies life to the point of glory.'

Nan Shepherd, *The Living Mountain*

Aiguille du Midi

PREFACE

Like many iconic mountains, Mont Blanc and its surrounding massif has long fascinated those of us who love to explore high places. Sometimes, such a mountain is also sacred, never climbed, so this fascination is not always simply about scaling its peaks.

While I've never actually climbed Mont Blanc, it is fair to say that it has captivated me over the years. I saw its summit for the first time, soaring high above the cloud, when as a student I arrived in Chamonix on the overnight coach from London. Until then I had not seen mountains so high. I can still recall that thrill.

This book is an account of a wonderful trip I had running the Tour du Mont Blanc in the summer of 2014 and follows on from my first book, *Adventures in Mind*. A version of chapter seven formed my contribution to *Waymaking*. It is a celebration of what my journeys in the mountains mean to me and how they inspire me. I am still exploring why I do this – and as long as I keep learning, I probably always will be.

The Balmat and Saussure statue in central Chamonix

CHAPTER
ONE

In the summer holiday after my first year at uni, I climbed some classic beginner's Alpine routes with friends. In between bouts of heavy rain, these climbs included the Index on the Aiguille Rouge, the North East Ridge on the Aiguille de l'M, the Cosmiques Arête on the Aiguille du Midi and a snow plod up the Mont Blanc du Tacul. For those last two climbs we spent a few nights camping on the Vallee Blanche, the great snow-covered glacier high on the massif. This in itself was an incredible experience – 3,800m higher than I had ever been before. It showed me what stark beauty, excitement and thrills were to be found in high-level mountaineering. Aged nineteen, I was already absorbed in climbing, loving it for its adventure, challenge and rebellious nature. After that first trip to the Alps I was completely hooked.

I had planned to return to Chamonix the following summer, but did not. Two of my friends died climbing on Mont Blanc a few weeks before I was due to leave. This tragedy showed how dangerous Alpine climbing can be. It made me question my own capabilities as a climber. It made me question whether the risks are too great. I do not believe they are and I did not stop climbing. Since then, however, I have rarely climbed in the high mountains.

While part of this is certainly because of the loss of my friends, there are other reasons. Over the years I had become drawn into cycling and running. At university I started fell running. Shortly after finishing my degree and starting my first job I got my first road bike. Climbing has always been there, but not in the all-encompassing way it was in my late teens and early twenties. I still occasionally go bouldering and do the odd long mountain route. I always enjoy these and perhaps in time I will climb more again.

My early days as a climber are always with me: they were formative in so many ways. Hitching to the crags, bivvying wherever we could, climbing all day, tall tales over beers in the evening, forming lasting friendships with like-minded people. Times change and now, like most of us, I have more responsibilities and commitments. That's not to say I don't look back. I often crave the dirtbag life – basic, simpler, more the real me.

Since my first trip, I've kept heading back to Chamonix and the Mont Blanc massif – always in summer. The first time I returned was in August 2002 to meet up with my brother who was interrailing at the time and spend a few days mountain biking around the valley with him before heading across to Verbier in Switzerland for the Grand Raid Cristalp mountain bike race. This is a hard race – starting and finishing in the ski resorts of Verbier and Grimentz, it takes in superb mountain bike trails, is 130km long and has over 3,500m of climbing. It was the first time I'd really challenged myself with a long race and I was so nervous I almost didn't start. I now remember a long, hot, tough and beautiful day in the saddle. The exhilaration I felt on finishing gave me a confidence boost that spurred me onwards for years. I rode the Grand Raid five more times, and usually spent at least a few days in and around Chamonix as part of each trip.

Mountain bike racing also took me to Bavaria, the Tirol and the Dolomites. I rode the Transalp mountain bike race three times, each year from 2003 when I was in my mid-twenties. This eight-day stage race starts in southern Germany and travels to Austria, Switzerland and Italy, crossing the mountains to finish at Riva del Garda. This was the race that opened my eyes to other parts of the Alps and how these mountains change in their look, feel and beauty with their geology and geography.

Despite my increased awareness of the size and scale of this mountain range, I still felt the pull to the Chamonix valley. In the summer of 2005 I spent a week with my partner Aidan in Les Houches, running, cycling and climbing. Three years later I spent some time there with friends Anna and Chez Frost – part of a training trip to the Haute-Savoie we made a month or so before we raced the Saab Salomon MountainX adventure race.

Being possibly too attracted to Chamonix meant I didn't travel further afield in the Alps, but the Saab Salomon MountainX race helped me spread my wings. The route of this five-day adventure race went along the French side of the Mont Blanc Massif, from Bourg-Saint-Maurice to Morzine, and many wonderful places in between. My eyes were opened to the beauty and variation of the Savoie and Haute Savoie Alpine regions – Beaufortain and Aravis, the Samoëns valley and the Chablis Alps. In July the following year I cycled around the 210-mile road version of the Tour du Mont Blanc, raced the Alpe d'Huez triathlon and cycled in the Chablis Alps and Aravis region. That September I went back again and cycled around much more of the French Alps, riding from Lake Geneva to Nice and back again via the Savoie, the Ecrins National Park, Maritime, Haute Provence, Drome, Vercors and Chartreuse regions. This was part of the Cent Cols Challenge – a cyclosportive of ten days that took a small group of riders on a memorable journey. During those 10 days we cycled over 100 alpine cols, riding on average 120 miles a day, seeing and visiting some wonderful places as well as testing our bodies to the limit. It was an amazing, absorbing time, from which I have many lasting memories – cresting the Col de Madeleine, the Turini in the rain, reaching the top of Mont Ventoux on a perfect blue-sky September morning and arriving at the Vercors plateau in the mist much later that same day, fatigued to the point of physical and mental exhaustion, but at the same time wholly exhilarated by my day's ride and the journey I was on.

Most of my visits to the Alps were driven by racing; whether training or racing I always seemed to need a reason, some goal to be aiming for. However, at some point in 2009 my mindset began to change. I'd enjoyed the solo ride around the Tour de Mont Blanc and the low-key nature of the Cent Cols Challenge much more than I'd enjoyed the heavily sponsored and hyped Alpe d'Huez Triathlon. Realising this told me I'd changed, but why?

Two books I read around this time probably had the most influence on this shift in my thinking. Walter Bonatti's *The Mountains of My Life* and Nan Shepherd's *The Living Mountain*. From the outset these two people seem quite different. Bonatti was one of the most driven, accomplished and principled mountaineers ever and Shepherd was an academic and writer who lived her life on the edge of Aberdeen, close to her beloved Cairngorms, where she spent many days and nights, moving across and into the mountains. After reading their books, I came to think that – despite their differences – these writers shared strong similarities in at least some of their characteristics.

But for both of them, a love of mountains seemed to be their guiding purpose. Each respected the mountains not as things to be beaten, but places in which to simply be – to become absorbed in. This seemed to come naturally to Shepherd, a state of mind she harboured her whole life. For Bonatti, however, it is arguable that this understanding of mountains as more than just a testing ground came later, when in his physical prime he turned his back on his extreme, audacious solo new-routing, turning instead to photography and writing, travelling the world to wild and remote places, recording the images he saw and writing about his experiences along the way.

Both Shepherd and Bonatti wrote about mountains in a spiritual way, in a manner that made me think about my own experiences out in the hills, question why I love them so, and to go about exploring myself and other places for the answer. This has taken me in many directions, some of which are obvious, and others not so. In doing so it has led me to explore creativity itself.

Creativity takes many forms. Some are obvious – painting, photography, writing – 'the arts'. But mathematics is also a creative subject. For some, this may not seem obvious – the logic required to add up, to follow some algorithm or other, is not a creative process. However, to be able to do new things in mathematics, or to be able to use established methods to solve novel or different problems, requires the ability to abstract the problem and to have an intuitive sense of what will work. Proof is subsequently required to back up this intuitive thinking – to show that the proposed solution logically makes sense. Mathematics is perhaps a key example of how logical thinking and creativity can form wonderful new things. Mathematicians at the leading edge of their subject certainly have to have the capacity to think in both of these ways, and to combine them together.

This aspect of creativity is something I've had significant experience of in the workplace as well as in my research – I've always worked full-time alongside studying. Perversely there was next to no requirement for creativity during my first mathematics degree, probably one of the main reasons I did badly and stopped studying for the most of the subsequent decade. However, I never stopped wanting to explore it more. In some ways I did so in my work as a software developer and my continued desire to learn pushed me to start studying for a Statistics MSc in 2005, which I finished in 2008. A year after that I started a PhD. My work and PhD research were closely linked. Both require innovative thinking and the ability to solve computational problems in order to analyse large datasets and identify their underlying messages – to find the signals in the noise. My skills and experience in this area have become more relevant with the so-called advent of 'big data'. Whether big or not, I find data interesting and challenging intellectually. These days there's even a profession that describes my combination of skills – I am a data scientist.

In 2014, I set up my own consultancy and software design company. While I'd always thought I would do this some day, I didn't think I'd do it so soon – but I'd moved to a new job that didn't work out. I joined a company as Chief Intelligence Officer, a grandiose job title under which I was promised the time and space to innovate and develop ideas that the company could exploit commercially. I quit early, just under three months in. Far from giving me creative space, I found I was stifled, expected to solve some big problems created before I joined. Having already done similar things for previous employers I could have solved those problems, but I had no interest in going over old ground. No matter what they paid me, I would learn nothing new. And it may sound naive, but I could not reconcile myself to a relentless drive to make money – the company had no other ethos. I'd begun my career in the private sector and then spent twelve years in the public sector before starting this new job. My brief failed stint back in a highly commercial environment affirmed my need for something more than just money to work for.

I left the company by literally cycling off into the sunset on a little folding bicycle, late on a Tuesday afternoon in early spring. While that may sound romantic, it was not. Like many people I had a mortgage and other financial commitments, and I had Alanna, my two-year-old daughter, so I was taking a pretty big risk. Fortunately, I picked up some work after a month or so and more followed. Self-employment gave me more of the autonomy I craved but the flip side was the risk of not being able to sustain an income, which initially led me to take on too much work. I managed to get it all done, but it was a challenging and stressful time.

In the midst of all this sprang a strong desire to get out in the mountains. I found the levels of work and thinking I needed to do intense, and began to crave a little time away to relax and refresh myself. My partner Aidan and I had agreed after I'd quit the new job that we would each take a few short trips away from home that year, either with friends or on our own. Ideally these trips would have been together, but neither of us wanted to leave our daughter without one of us around for more than a day or so, and we didn't want to spend too long away from home.

Aidan had been steadily ticking off all of Scotland's Munros, and would use his time off to bag some more. For me, I planned a few days running in the Scottish Highlands with Andrea Priestley, a friend I'd met in 2004 at the Pentland 5 hill race near Edinburgh. Despite living some distance away, having moved to the edge of Stirling in Scotland from Ilkley, six miles down the road from Otley, she'd stayed in my running club – the Ilkley Harriers, so we'd kept in touch. Aidan and I also often stay with Andrea and her husband Mark on our way up to holidays in the Highlands – they are good friends.

I'd also run the Calderdale Way relay fell race with her. I found it a world of pain. In fell race relays, pairs of racers from the same club run together over a number of sections of the whole race route. Andrea and I ran the hilliest section of the route together and I strained to keep in touch with her over the ten miles or so we had to cover. The night before the relay, Andrea, Mark, an academic at Stirling University, and their daughter Megan, had stayed at my house. Over dinner we had lots more conversation and heated debates about many things. Both of them goaded me, saying I'd be certain to begin a PhD after the MSc I was working hard to complete. At that time I was jaded by studying, and strongly believed an MSc would be enough. They were, however, right and two years later I started a PhD.

I saw Andrea once or twice a year at fell race relays. In October 2009, I ran with her (and again suffered) in the Ian Hodgson Mountain Relay in the Lake District and we agreed to race the Original Mountain Marathon (OMM) together later that month. Since then we have raced many mountain marathons together, as well as had numerous trips out running in the Lake District and Scottish Highlands. It is fair to say that I feel daunted by Andrea – she is a very talented mountain runner, borne out by her becoming British fell running champion in 2002. She is also someone who has strong opinions that she holds with conviction. When we run together in the mountains we have many long conversations. One of our first was about the state of mathematical education; as a part-time teacher and social worker carrying out research in education, she had well-formed opinions I found interesting and thought-provoking. But we discuss all kinds of things while we're out on the hill and laugh a lot. Equally, we are comfortable with saying little to each other – something more likely to happen when we are racing together or when we each retreat into our own little worlds of thought as we climb or run along a hillside.

We pencilled this trip in for late spring – before the midges arrived. In early April, however, I was hit with bad flu and it took me two months or so to recover enough to be able to do long days of mountain running. June came around and we started planning again. We were going to head to some wonderful wild and mountainous places in the Highlands but it was a wet summer and high season for midges, which would likely have made the camping we had planned miserable. An alternative plan began to hatch early one morning as I ran between Alanna's nursery and where I was working in central Leeds. I realised it had been some time since I had been to the Alps.

After becoming parents, most of our family holidays were spent in the Lake District and Scottish Highlands so we did get our time in mountainous places. But not the Alps. As soon as I thought of it I started planning. Alanna was in a nursery four days a week, so I spent Fridays with her and I didn't want to miss this. I figured a flight out to Geneva on a Sunday evening, returning the following Thursday evening, would give us four days to run the route. After checking flight times and finding it would definitely work, I texted Andrea. She was up for it too. Later that day Aidan heard my plan with amused resignation – he could see how excited I was. And that was that, we were going – and in less than three weeks.

Andrea and I had both run around the Tour du Mont Blanc before. Andrea a number of times as she is ten years older than me. She and Mark did it first in 1993 as a means of getting fit for their summer of alpine climbing. I'd run the route in July 2010. It was a wonderful experience that helped me get my head back together after an eventful cycling trip to Canada and the USA. So I was looking forward to a long run in the Alps, staying in mountain refuges, heading back to somewhere I love.

The last time I'd been there I'd only just started painting. This time I would take my camera, record some of the scenes we saw so I could paint them in the ensuing months. I find painting the places I have been wholly absorbing – it's almost like I return to them, the way I was feeling, the time of day, all the memories come flooding back. At the same time I am lost in my attempt to capture the scene in a painting, a different headspace to the places I find myself when in the mountains, writing or carrying out research, but one I have now come to value as much as these other three.

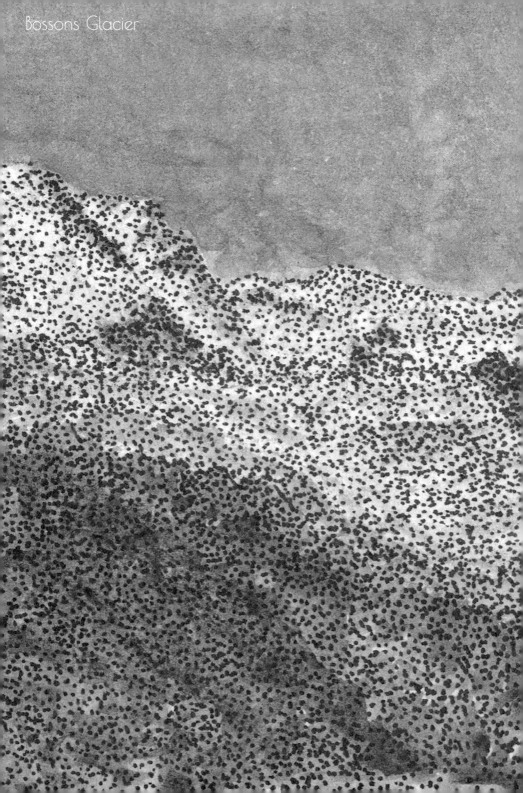
Bossons Glacier

CHAPTER
TWO

July 13th 2014. It was a week after the Grand Départ of the Tour de France had visited Yorkshire and left the county with great memories of what was probably its most amazing weekend of sport ever. I'd been in Otley with friends and family and the race passed through the town centre soon after it had started in central Leeds. The following day the race started in York, passing less than ten miles north of Otley as it headed west to meet the Pennines and follow them south to the Peak District and eventually Sheffield. I saw it again having cycled out with my brother Mike to Kex Gill near Blubberhouses, the high point of the road between York and Skipton. The atmosphere during both of these days had been superb. It felt like the whole county had come together to celebrate both the race and the beauty and challenge of Yorkshire's terrain. There was a proudness that was palpable, something that felt great to be part of.

Over the weekend of the race, the roads it took were closed to all cars other than race support vehicles. After the race had passed over Kex Gill, Mike and I headed west down the York to Skipton road – usually busy with fast-moving traffic. We were in company with thousands of other cyclists, all different ages, shapes and sizes on all different kinds of pushbikes. Not only had we just seen the world's biggest cycle race going over our home roads, for a brief, fantastic time we cyclists owned those roads. After Yorkshire, the race headed south to London and the following day it was in France. Quite soon the Tour would reach the Alps, but Andrea and I would get there sooner.

When we met at Manchester Airport it was the third time I had seen Andrea that year. In May we'd cycled the English Coast to Coast, and in June run the Lowe Alpine Mountain Marathon (LAMM) in Glen Carron in the north-west Highlands. We'd already done pretty well for trips but were still very happy to be at the start of this, our next adventure.

We met at the airport in the late afternoon, checked in, got through departures and then went for a coffee to catch up. Each of us had a jam-packed 15-litre rucksack. That was it, no other baggage. While we did think about taking a larger bag of extra clean clothes and other niceties for before and after doing the Tour de Mont Blanc, we decided against it – it would take extra time both at the airport and we'd have to sort out somewhere to leave it in Chamonix.

We successfully connected with our shuttle bus after our flight to Geneva. The driver was English and based in Chamonix. He said the weather had been poor and, despite the fact it was July, he'd been walking around town for the last few weeks in his down jacket. However, he reassured us by saying it was due to improve over the next day or so. We arrived at our hotel in Les Bossons, a few miles down the valley from Chamonix centre, at about half past ten that evening.

It was the night of the World Cup final between Germany and Argentina. The hotel had the match on a big screen by the bar, surrounded by some very enthusiastic Germans. Happy for them and their team's win, we had a swift beer and went to bed. Not to sleep all that well, though, as I was too excited. I was up early the following morning, busying myself with final bits of packing and raring to get going.

Early next morning it felt fresh after the night's heavy rain. There was a chill in the air and the cloud was low on the mountaintops. We left the hotel and followed the road that took us to a bridge over the Arve and onto an off-road trail that we followed for a few miles down river to Les Houches. Given that it was dark when we arrived in the valley the night before, this was the first glimpse I had of the valley this visit.

I will always remember the very first time that I saw it, a young aspiring climber full of excitement and bravado-edged fear. In her inspiring autobiography *The Space Below My Feet*, Gwen Moffat – Britain's first female mountain guide – describes the first time she saw these mountains.

> **First the gleam of them, with the sun full on the vast fields, no shadows, and brightness which, in that first great moment, seemed cloud above. And then I realised it wasn't cloud, that it was all snow, solid, tangible matter reared upwards, so unbelievably high that, for an infinitesimal moment, one had the sensation of physical effort as the eye struggled still higher to reach the summit. To one who had never seen a peak higher than Ben Nevis, Mont Blanc, in that first awakening, was perfection.**

On reading Moffat's words, almost two decades after I first saw Mont Blanc, I wholly understood them because I had felt the same. I remember craning my head, having to look even higher than I had anticipated to see the summit, almost not believing a mountain could look so high. Moffat captures a naive fascination with the Mont Blanc massif that others have expressed in different ways. There is a well-known statue in the main square of Chamonix of Jacques Balmat and his benefactor Horace Benedict de Saussure. Balmat was a Chamonix-based crystal collector who, with local doctor Michel-Gabriel Paccard in 1786, was the first to successfully reach the summit of Mont Blanc. Saussure was the financier who funded their climb. It is an evocative statue – looking at it you can feel Balmat's excitement and passion as he points to the mountain encouraging Saussure, telling him the summit is within his reach.

Chamonix is in a hanging valley – to reach it you must climb up from the town of Sallanches in a the lower and wider stretch of the Arve valley, or cross over from Switzerland's Sion valley over the Col des Montets. I think this is part of what makes it feel special – a sense of disconnect from elsewhere, and the fact that in the valley you are surrounded on almost all sides by beautiful mountains steeped in the history of Alpine mountaineering. Like many others I first arrived in town an aspirant climber, wanting to climb the walls, crags and peaks where some of the greatest had cut their teeth.

The town centre is always a bustling place, a commercial hub that feels a long way away from the mountains that surround it. Besides the tourists and the well to do, there are mountain bikers, walkers and runners, but perhaps most special is the erratic stream of climbers heading down off the hill after their multi-day epics. You can always recognise them. Big boots, heavy packs with ice axes and ropes strapped to the outside. Unkempt, sweaty, bleary-eyed with tiredness, and carrying a more general weariness from their nights out on the mountain having adventures. I always envy them that. I still remember the thirst I carried off the hill after our few nights camping on the Vallee Blanche – probably the strongest I had ever encountered – the subsequent drink from a fountain of cool, fresh water among the most satisfying.

Since my first visit to Chamonix I have returned many times. I love to sit in the square, gazing up at the massif, basking in it all. During this trip, our shortest day's running would be our final day, from the Col de la Forclaz in Switzerland to Chamonix. We hoped to finish by lunchtime and spend a few hours relaxing in the sun before heading back to Geneva to catch our flight back to Manchester.

So I was back, after a few years and some big changes in my life. This was a trip to be savoured. As well as enjoying the run I wanted to bask in the scenery, to take pictures that would enable me to relive the moments when I painted them back home in Yorkshire. I would only be there for four days and I wanted to stretch them out, to make them last longer using memories.

The village of Les Bossons sits below the Bossons glacier, which plunges down the mountainside from side of Mont Blanc. The glacier has a blue tinge to its whiteness, its shape a distinct and beautiful feature on the mountainside, something I always look to and remember, whatever I happen to be doing.

Gazing at the glacier and wondering whether it is the activity or the aesthetic that is more important to me to these days – and coming to the conclusion that I would not want to choose one above the other – led me to think about an article published in issue 29 of the mountaineering journal *Alpinist*. Ed Douglas was interviewing the climber Andy Parkin. Entitled *A Muscular Imagination – Andy Parkin and the Art of Climbing*, the article focuses on Parkin, a climber and mountaineer in his fifties from Douglas's hometown of Sheffield who now lives in Chamonix. He works as an artist, finding inspiration in his local mountains and travelling around the world (notably to the granite peaks and spires of Patagonia), both climbing – new routing – and seeking to further develop his creative thought. Parkin was explaining to Douglas his feelings about mountains.

'The *how* is so important in climbing,' Parkin tells me, drinking tea outside his studio the next day. 'It's the reason we do it. It's gratifying to be successful, to have ambitions and all that. But the actual execution has got to be as pure ethically as I can make it. Otherwise, there's no point. I don't ever want to become complacent about anything. For fear of losing that creative edge, not the sporting one.

'I know a lot of climbers who don't necessarily love the mountains,' he continues. 'They love the activity, the sport. But it's not the same love as someone who really loves the mountains, every aspect from the moraine to the brooks or streams at the bottom. Their moods.'

When I first read the article, I remembered a photograph of Parkin I had seen many times around fifteen years earlier in a rock climbing guidebook. He is climbing London Wall, a classic hard crack line on Millstone Edge. In the Peak District, close to the natural gritstone edges of Stanage and Burbage, Millstone is one of the finest quarried gritstone edges in the UK. Classic crack climbs abound at all grades; one of my earliest dalliances with a Hard Very Severe graded climb was the brilliant Great North Road, on the Embankment Wall area of the crag.

Douglas's piece discusses how, during the 1970s and 1980s, Parkin extended his mountaineering experiences beyond the Peak District gritstone edges of his youth, to new and hard climbs in the Greater Ranges. The aesthetic is always important to Parkin; his climbing had, and still maintains, a vision and an elegance that is reflected in his new routes, and in his sculpture and painting. His new routes and the style in which he repeats existing climbs are an extension of his artistry: sculpting, painting and climbing are one and the same. As he says in the above quote, the style of execution of a climb is at least as important to him as the achievement of that climb; it's not about ticking off the route, writing it down in some logbook.

The clean crack lines of Millstone are examples of climbs that are obvious. First ascentionists of these cracks would have the challenge and pleasure of being the first to climb the plumb line, and the associated honour of naming the new route. They would not, however, have had to use their imagination, creativity or canniness as a climber or mountaineer in any way when devising the route. There's nothing wrong with that – there is much to be said for simplicity within elegance –obvious climbs often form the classic route of a rock face precisely because of their elegant simplicity. Many climbers would not care or even give a passing thought to the relevance and beauty of this – it's a climb, just do it. No doubt they will enjoy the climb, but perhaps they miss one of the fundamental reasons why the climb is so enjoyable: its simplicity.

I took away the impression from Douglas's fine article that Parkin achieves a feat that some climbers endeavour to replicate, but few fully attain – the new lines he climbs on his travels to the Himalaya, Andes and beyond are at times complex, but always maintain an elegance through vision, creativity and a strong sense of ethics. To do this takes principles, sheer determination and drive. Douglas discusses how Parkin found at least some of this drive while recovering from a life-threatening fall: 'The near-fatal accident that he suffered in 1984 may have changed Parkin's physical capabilities, but it also pushed him to discover a singular and creative edge.' Climbing on the Riffelhorn above Zermatt in Switzerland, Parkin's belay failed. The injuries he sustained in the subsequent fall should have killed him. Today he is left with a pronounced limp and an enhanced determination.

Parkin maintains this 'singular and creative edge' because he doesn't view the mountains merely as a place to go for sport; he views them as a place to 'be'. His climbing, art, and the mountains are intertwined. It is here he gets many of his ideas, his inspiration and, at times, the physical material he sculpts. The article recounts how he collects from the bottom of a glacier above Chamonix, some of the metal remnants of a mountain refuge long destroyed. Once an integral part of an at times life-saving shelter, these remnants had been chewed up, transported down the valley, then spat out by the river of ice. A photograph in the article shows one of his sculptures that incorporates this material, temporarily installed on the Mer de Glace glacier above Chamonix. While it is out of context, it fits in this place, a form of beauty developed from waste, disorder and creativity, surrounded by natural beauty. I found a resonance in Douglas's piece for *Alpinist* that extended beyond physical mountains and their climbing: the process is as important as the outcome.

This process can be so many things, but is it everything? The care and attention devoted to the way something is done – the 'how' as Parkin says – may not necessarily influence the material perception of the end product, but it can certainly enhance both the quality of the outcome and the satisfaction of the person or people completing the task. That is the difference between mass-production and the work of craftsmen and women. A bookcase is a bookcase whether it's assembled from a flat-pack or designed and built for its place from carefully selected material by a skilled cabinetmaker. While both fulfil their required role, the quality of the latter is likely to shine through in its aesthetics and longevity and I know which of the two I would prefer in my house. Of course, you generally have to pay a price for quality – in time, money or both. The quick and dirty or the considered and valued is a frequent decision in all areas of life, if you are lucky (wealthy) enough to be in the position where it is a choice.

Although the interview recounted the attitude of Andy Parkin to his climbing and his art, you can relate it to running, perhaps especially to mountain running and – maybe even more so given the location and terrain you run over – in following the route of the Tour du Mont Blanc.

In recent years, running terminology has been updated to recognise the increase in races that go beyond the twenty-six miles of a marathon. And sometimes far beyond those twenty-six miles, as the rise of 'ultra-running' has arisen as a separate discipline. One of the first major races to stimulate its establishment, the 105-mile Ultra-Trail du Mont Blanc (UTMB) is one of the most popular and iconic races of its kind in the world. Demand for entries is huge and, since its inception, the number of people running the course of the TMB has increased massively.

I lost count of how many people asked us if we were training for the Ultra-Trail du Mont Blanc when we were either running or resting at one of the mountain huts we stayed in overnight. No, we weren't! It's not that this was an unreasonable assumption, just that the purpose we were running the TMB was not to train for a race but to immerse and challenge ourselves in an immensely beautiful environment. You don't always need to be training for something.

In 2010 I had an entry for the UTMB, part of the reason I ran around it earlier that summer was to recce it. That time around, I finished it injured with an Achilles tendon problem that lasted beyond the actual race in August. However, I realised during running the route that I was not sure if I ever would want to race it. That may be due to its length and toughness. I also found that spending a few days to do it, staying in mountain huts, getting tired but not to the point of hallucination, having the time and the capacity to take in the beauty as well as run the trails at my own pace, was a far more appealing means of doing it.

This is probably at least in some part an age thing – ten years before I would have charged around as fast as I could without stopping to think about it. These kind of experiences in themselves can be incredible. With long-distance challenges, I find that when I have reached a kind of tipping point, beyond the physical, into more of a head game, I become almost displaced from my surroundings, in my own little world. It may sound perverse (and a bit weird), but I do like that little world. It's a challenging, at times mind-blowing place, but I find out more about myself there. It's also an abstract place – somewhere to escape to, where I still feel in the present, but disassociated from immediate reality. I used to try to get to it as much as I could through physical challenges. I am still addicted to going there, at times I yearn to take myself there. However, I've come to realise that there are other routes to this abstract place than pushing myself really hard physically, and if I try to spend all my time in it I will miss out on other valuable experiences.

Being with Andrea meant I got to hear stories from her own many visits to the Chamonix valley, her ascents of Mont Blanc, climbing some of the classics, trips around the Tour du Mont Blanc and other long distance routes with her husband. During one of her earlier experiences of running the TMB, back in the early 1990s, she and Mark encountered a mountain guide at a hut who chastised them for wearing fell running shoes instead of big walking boots. How times change! They were just ahead of the game; these days trail running shoes are the norm, along with compression clothing and ubiquitous Euro-styled Lycra. I wonder what that mountain guide would make of it now – would he shrug his shoulders in bemusement and stick with his usual kit or join in with the crowd?

We had a breakfast of pain au raisin in the village. Not for the first time on a trip with Andrea, I found she had a knack for finding a good patisserie. I just to leave her to it at breakfast time – she will always find good coffee, bread and cake – caffeine and calories to charge the start of our days on the hill. The trail we would follow from Les Bossons would take us to a bridge where we would recross the river to reach Les Houches. This is one of the traditional start points for the Tour du Mont Blanc, and it is here that we would join the route proper.

We were heading to the Refuge des Mottets in the Vallee de Glaciers. This mountain hut is at the foot of the Aiguille de Glaciers, a 3,817m peak situated on the south-western flank of the Mont Blanc massif. This would be around 25 miles and 2,000 metres ascent, enough for our first day. We were not all that bothered about trying to run all that fast (or at least I wasn't), but we did have an ambition to get to the different huts we were staying in each evening in time to have a shower and a little relaxing reading before dinner. This was our only time pressure and it was enough. While we didn't have time to dawdle, we didn't have to completely nail it either.

The mountain hut network in the Alps is brilliant. At the end of the day you can stop, grab a shower, dinner, a bed for the night and breakfast the following morning. All this is done alongside others who are on their own Alpine travels, having their own adventures, making for a great atmosphere in the evening at dinner in particular, as stories are shared and likely embellished as the wine begins to flow.

The rain was clearing, but we could see we were in for a mixed day. From Les Houches the TMB climbs up to the Col de Voza, a saddle point on the north-eastern ridge of Mont Blanc that separates the Chamonix and Les Contamines valleys. The path climbs steeply out of Les Houches and stays pretty steep until the col, mostly following a ski run. I got the familiar daunting feeling I always get when beginning something mountainous and long – in a strange kind of way I really value this feeling and these days I don't get to experience it as often as I used to.

It didn't take long to get a view – we could see up and across the valley, though somewhat impeded by the low cloud. It is busy and built up; the Mont Blanc road tunnel brings much traffic. In the years after it was closed following the 1999 tragedy when a fire swept throughout killing 41 people, the valley was a quieter place. I remember during one trip running past the mouth of the empty tunnel and realising just how peaceful it was compared to when it was open. While it was closed there was a campaign by some locals to keep it shut for good. I could understand that, but the pressure to reopen one of the major routes between France and Italy proved too great and it reopened in 2003.

The Col de Voza is 1,650m, almost 1,000m lower than the highest point of the TMB, the Col des Fours, which we would reach later that day. As such it was a good warm-up with alpine meadow surrounding it above the treeline. That morning the col was quiet; we saw just a few other walkers as we reached the saddle point. It has a hotel, a station on the Mont Blanc railway and a cable car station, so I imagine it could get busier.

At the col was our first route choice – the TMB has numerous variants. We could drop into the Les Contamines valley and follow this low route all the way until the beginning of the climb up to the Col de Bonhomme, or stay a little higher, traversing the mountainside via the Col du Tricot to meet the lower route further up the valley, beyond the village of Les Contamines. This latter option had more climb and, given the weather conditions and our desire to get the first day in the bag, we opted for the lower of the two.

CHAPTER
THREE

Les Contamines

The trail dropped westwards off the hillside. We left the open meadow and were back in the pine trees – damp and green, smelling of forest – following a wide track that zigzagged down the hillside. The route of the TMB heads to the valley to follow the Bon Nant river up to and beyond the village of Les Contamines. We would continue to follow this river until close to its source, and then climb up to the Col de Bonhomme at the head of the valley. From there we would climb a little further to the Col de Bonhomme de Croix and then a little further still to the Col des Fours, after which was a descent down into the Vallee des Glaciers. At 2,665m the Col des Fours is one of the high points of the whole TMB route. Given the weather we thought we'd be in for a bit of a drenching up here, and we hoped the snow line wouldn't be too troublesome. Going lightweight meant we hadn't brought any of the crampons or walking poles that are helpful on snow that is tricky to traverse.

Quickly we were down in the valley, running along a path by the river. We could see the saddle of the Col de Bonhomme up the valley, nestled between the cloud-covered tops of the Aiguilles de la Pennaz and the Tête Nord des Fours. To me it looked further away than the ten miles or so we had to reach it – one of those landmarks that seems distant until you're almost upon it.

The path by the river was muddy – a little sticky with puddles in places, more than anything reminding me of my local trails back home in Wharfedale. While the mud felt the same, the setting was not – Alpine chalets lined our route, and the hills surrounding us felt bigger, even though we could not see them fully, shrouded in mist as they were. Seeing the chalets and low alpine meadow along the valley floor, I recalled how I'd been missing my adventures in them, spending time instead just remembering them. As we ran towards Les Contamines, it suddenly hit me that I really was there, and would be for the following few days, running over some beautiful Alpine terrain, spending my evenings and nights up high, sleeping in the places I'd been dreaming about.

It feels hard for me to express in ways that do not seem materialistic and selfish, but I need long days in the mountains. And I mean *need* and not *want* – these days help me to stay sane. I need to feel myself fade into unimportance, surrounded by the imposing beauty that brings it all into perspective. Whether cycling, running, climbing – it's not really the sporting activity that's important to me, but the process of challenging myself and in being surrounded by wild mountains. I need the challenge as well as the beauty... it helps me to really feel alive.

In her book *The Fish Ladder*, Katharine Norbury explores this urge – this love – that she and others have for different places. For her the place is the Llŷn Peninsula in North Wales.

> **Love. I wasn't sure about it. But the feeling of longing, or yearning for something not quite discernible that could almost be nostalgia. A sense that this was acute as hunger, or homesickness, but not necessarily for a place that one knew. Something elusive, unquantifiable, and yet – in its very depth and poignancy – as compelling as desire.**

While Norbury's book is about many things, it is centred around her journeys following the course of different rivers – from their mouths at the sea to their sources up in the hills. The thing that she is seeking at each source is not physically discernible – these are journeys she feels compelled to do in a bid to find healing for her troubled mind.

Norbury was inspired to travel to the beginnings of rivers by the Scottish writer Neil Gunn. In his books *The Well at the World's End* and *Highland River*, Gunn writes in spiritual, mythical ways of such journeys to upland river sources. Set in the Scottish Highlands, these two books are evocative of the wild beauty and peace to be found there.

In the year before this trip, I read two other books that describe similar journeys. In *White River* and *Wild Voices*, Jamie Whittle and Mike Cawthorne write of their separate experiences of exploring the River Findhorn, from the Moray Firth on the east coast of Scotland up into its beginnings in the Monadhliath Mountains – the grey hills to the north-west of the Cairngorms. Whittle and Cawthorne were also inspired by Gunn – Cawthorne more explicitly so, as Gunn's is the 'wild voice' that he explores as he makes his journey.

In their books none of these three writers find anything physical at the end of their journey, but that's not what they're looking for. Each of the narratives is compelling because of what they find in themselves, and in how they evoke and celebrate the landscape surrounding them as they do so. None of this work is repetitive – Norbury, Whittle and Cawthorne have their own, individual voices but each has a need to seek, to explore themselves and to find solace surrounded by nature and wild places. In travelling to the source of a river, the landscape inevitably becomes less controlled and more natural the further you get. The river is a metaphor – the three of them (and Gunn) are leaving society behind and returning to the wild.

Like Norbury, Cawthorne, Whittle and Gunn, many others have explored this need. It is in them as it is in me. With the current rise in 'new nature writing' it is easy to think that this is a recent phenomenon – that it's a reaction to the confused, incoherent state of our society. That may be so to a degree, but in truth I think this kind of writing is ages old. Writing about wild places and nature, the pull we feel to them and what they evoke in us, is similar if not the same as the writing of high, rugged, lonely, risky places as found in mountaineering literature. They share the same natural root – Robert Macfarlane's *Mountains of the Mind* and *The Wild Places* reflects this, and Nan Shepherd connects the two when in *The Living Mountain* she writes of a climber friend who cares little for racing up mountains but who loves to climb in them: 'What he values is a task that, demanding of him all he has and is, absorbs and so releases him entirely.'

Look to the work of Henry Thoreau, Walt Whitman, Ralph Waldo Emerson and their peers, and you will find writers who did the same kind of exploration almost 200 years ago. When I began reading some of the work of this group of writers – the American Transcendentalists – I started with *Nature*, Emerson's seminal work, in which he discussed his own philosophy on how he believed individuals should see, attempt to understand and to interact with both their internal and external worlds.

Nature was published in 1836, at a time when the country that is now the USA was discovering and establishing a cultural and intellectual identity of its own. A young country in the eyes of those who had settled in it. Emerson believed it was not necessary to look to the past, to the cultures of Europe, the places from which those early settlers arrived to develop the desired identity, it could be found by looking to nature and the science underpinning it, in each individual living and treating others with respect, in each person having an integrity, a unique identity, that was borne from natural – not material – values.

Central to Emerson's beliefs was what nature and returning to it has the capacity to do for the individual, that seeing and being in nature is self-restoring.

> To the body and mind which have been cramped by noxious work or company, nature is medicinal and restores their tone. The tradesman, the attorney comes out of the din and craft of the street and sees the sky and the woods, and is man again. In their eternal calm, he finds himself. The health of the eye seems to demand a horizon. We are never tired, so long as we can see far enough.

Emerson was so right. The change in routine to one that is more simple and straightforward is always refreshing for me, and another reason why I feel a pull to the mountains. As Emerson's words show, it is nothing new, and is something many people feel a compulsion to do, at least in the last few hundred years as increasingly in society we have gained the headspace and the leisure time to do so. Heading out from a world of industry and the artificial to places of nature and wildness is widely recognised as something that is consoling and rejuvenating.

One morning while writing this book I was on a train travelling along the Settle-Carlisle line through the Yorkshire Dales. Heading for Garsdale Head near Kirkby Stephen, I planned to ride my mountain bike back to Settle along the Pennine Bridleway. It was a beautiful cold and clear Sunday morning in January and the train was full of people heading out to walk in Dales. Since the railway line was built in 1874, people from cities of Leeds, Bradford and Carlisle have used it to get out to the hills. While there is a sense of nostalgia in doing the same now, I don't think the reasons we do it have changed.

> The people setting out on these walks weren't seeking to conquer peaks or test themselves against maps and miles. They were looking for a mystical communion with the land; they walked backwards in time to an imagined place suffused with magical, native glamour: to Merrie England, or to pre-historic England, pre-industrial visions that offered solace and safety to sorely troubled minds. For though railways and roads and a burgeoning market in countryside books had contributed to this movement, at heart it had grown out of the trauma of the Great War, and was flourishing in fear of the next.

Helen MacDonald's thoughts from *H is for Hawk* discuss how in the 1930s thousands of people walked across the South Downs by night, and her theories on why they did it. It seemed serendipitous that I read these words for the first time as I was taking the train out to Garsdale – they certainly resonated with me at the time. There was a palpable feeling of excitement on the train – it was a perfect blue-sky winter morning, and many of its passengers were heading out to a place of beauty to spend their Sunday. Later, as I rode my bike along the trails, surrounded by the scenery of the Dales, I thought about Emerson's and MacDonald's words. Are we still clinging on to the same things as those people were in the 1930s and the 1870s?

While my own and my parents' generation are lucky not to have lived through two world wars, we do live with plenty of uncertainty – much of which is created by ourselves and society. I don't know if the expectations that society places on us are any more pressured than they were back in the thirties. There is certainly pressure to conform, to blend in, to follow the crowd. At least that's what I find. I think I am forever seeking autonomy – I want to do things my own way. Some of the time that might be the wrong way, but failure is one of the best ways to learn. That the choices we make and the lives we lead are not wholly autonomous is something I find frustrating, sometimes so much so I could despair if it weren't for my routes back to my preferred reality.

Getting away enables relaxation and reflection (although this might seem quite a perverse thing to say for a long-distance run). This is so important to me. It could be a run of thirty minutes or twelve hours, but I value it all the same. And why running rather than walking? I love the physical exertion and the free, fast movement of running. Getting the blood flowing oxygen around my body feels good and there is no doubt that I am addicted to the endorphin kick. Practically I suppose I run because it's quicker than walking – I cover more distance and ground. While doing the TMB I was 'time limited' – that might be a trite phrase, but one that reflects so many things about today's society. This is selfish in its most literal sense, and I don't deny that. There also needs to be a bit of space to be selfish – the 'self' is the most important part of us that not only forms who we are but how we are perceived and interact with others. I have an important and wonderful role now – that of mother. I also have a very supportive partner who understands my needs to get out into mountains and helps me to get into them. This keeps me balanced – enabling me to try to be the mother I want to be and to really appreciate the fortune I have to have a healthy family and two lovely little girls. My time in the mountains is, of course, less than it used to be, but I find I truly value the times I do now have in them, more so than before when I took them for me these days – I can reflect on them from my home or wherever I happen to be, and I love that. I can get absorbed and lost in trying to paint a mountain scene in much the same way I become absorbed by running across it. Both pastimes enable me to think in a different way, to look and to see.

Since becoming a parent I've become more aware of my own experiences of childhood and growing up, coming to realise further that they were actually pretty tough. I was always loved and cared for, but there was a continual shadow cast by my dad's mental health problems.

H is for Hawk is a wonderful book. It is one with very many threads, which MacDonald weaves together masterly, but what drove MacDonald to write it was the death of her father. She literally went mad with grief, finding therapy in training a goshawk. It will sound strange, but when I first started reading it I felt pangs of jealousy for MacDonald. I grieved for my dad for years, even when he was still alive. Living in a long-term care home in his late sixties, his mind tormented by decades of medication for various mental health problems, he had the body of someone twenty years older, steadily exacerbated by that same medication, his body degenerating as part of the process.

He was still the man he was, my dad, but that was so often hidden by layers of confusion and paranoia. I get so much of myself from him. When I visited him I could see that explicitly, in ways I couldn't when I was younger. I look so like him. He had a fierce intelligence although he always seemed fearful of it, even during his more lucid years. He spent his working life as an aerospace engineer. He loved the hills too, and understood that love in me, although he was always more wary of them than he should have been had he learned to truly trust a map and compass. I think I get at least part of my obsessive nature from him – he focused on one particular engineering formula for years, perhaps he thought he'd found a new way of doing something. He may well have done, but one of his problems was that he would never get to the end of something to find out if he was right or wrong. From that I have learned the importance of closing off things in my mind. I've had some interesting times doing that so far, and have come to realise that doing this is more important than whether I succeed or fail.

I think for years I was subconsciously scared that if I pursued the ideas that ran around my head, I would turn out like my dad. Instead I numbed them, pushing myself to the limit in the mountains to keep them quiet. They became increasingly resistant to this so I had to push harder and harder. Eventually I pushed myself so hard I broke during a mountain bike race across the USA. That was four years before this trip with Andrea. That race – the Tour Divide – begins in Banff in Canada. Closely following the line formed by the American Continental Divide south along the Rocky Mountains to the Mexican border, it finishes at Antelope Wells in New Mexico. It travels through 2,745 miles of some of the most beautiful and inspiring mountain landscapes in the world. This was a race I had dreamed about and trained hard for, hoping that it would be a perfect platform for me to use all the physical endurance and mental toughness I had acquired from a decade of doing long, hard races in the mountains. I wanted to see just how far I could go. In reality I didn't really get that far at all. I rode for four days and around 450 miles. With minimal, fitful sleep, a long way from home, and all by myself in the middle of Montana, I finally cracked.

Looking back now I know that those four days cycling through Canadian wilderness and under the big skies of Montana were some of my most formative. I rode over 110 miles a day on dirt trails, bivvying out on rough ground. While the physical toughness of the race contributed to my exhaustion, mentally I broke. I reached a point – a limit – where my body could have kept going but my mind just could not countenance doing so. I think I had been trying, subconsciously, to reach that point for a long time. Finally I had. In many ways it was a bleak place – exposing so many things about my self and my fallibilities to me. It was also a fundamentally honest place – I took a big hard look at myself and knew it was time to change. I left that race a quite different person to the one that started.

It would be great to be able to say that I faced off madness during that time in Montana. Of course I didn't. I came close to it, touched it, experienced it. I am still plenty fearful of it, and wholly respect it, but this experience helped me to realise that, if I did explore myself intellectually, what happened to my dad was not necessarily going to happen to me.

Today I am so glad I managed to break through. Since then I have explored myself further and found out so much more. Pushed myself in ways other than the physical and have gone on wonderful journeys doing so. They are not always comfortable journeys. I can still get close to the edge, needing self-awareness, empathy and love to make sure I get back. There is a real thrill to be found there, however – it's where true innovation lies.

There is, of course, a recognised link between creativity, obsession and insanity. One of the most famous examples of an artist with such gifts and

– so much so that he has come to symbolise the cliché of the tortured artist – is Vincent Van Gogh. Now judged highly influential and one of the creators of the post-impressionism movement, throughout his life as a painter he was viewed as a failure. During his frequent bouts of psychosis, he painted and painted, and painted. It must have been terribly hard to know that what you were doing was not recognised or believed in by your peers. Emotional torture which would have at least contributed to his suicide aged thirty-seven, if not been the main reason for it. History is littered with such tortured minds, people who pushed the boundaries in different fields and suffered mental instability along with pushing their innovations. In their lifetime not receiving the recognition they deserved because they were just too far ahead.

While this can all sound quite negative, the positives are also there. If experiencing insanity can contribute to the creation of fine art, new mathematics and other great ideas, then is it worth it? Poor Van Gogh killed himself. It was not worth it for him personally, mortal like the rest of us, even though in some ways he is now immortal. His is an extreme example, both in how he lived and in what he achieved. The outcomes of other people finding some of their most creative work when they are at their most mentally unstable are more common. Whatever it is induced by, the edge of insanity can be a powerful place.

H is for Hawk is a prime example of such an outcome. Writing this book must have been very therapeutic for MacDonald. It is a fine example of what a gifted person can do when exploring and recovering from going beyond the limits of her own sanity. I don't envy her the grief she had in that her father died. I envy her the reasons he left such a huge gap in her life. What happened to my dad over the years is a big, sad part of my life that sometimes leaps upon me unawares. One day when running into work I was suddenly overcome with a loud sobbing when, for the first time, I took proper time to consider the fact that my daughter will never really know or understand her granddad. That shocked me, not because of what it meant, but because I thought I had my emotions under greater control. The sobs stopped me in my stride.

The vibrancy of fatherhood is a beautiful and precious thing. This is something that my dad knew, and that my sister, brother and I lost a long time ago, when we were too young to realise what was going away.

Approaching the Col du Bonhomme

CHAPTER
FOUR

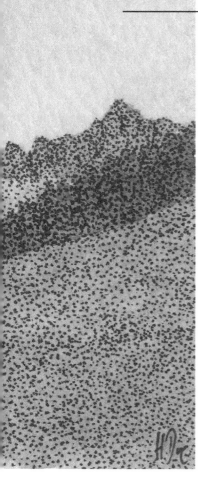

As we ran along the muddy path by the river, Andrea and I decided to stop for an early lunch in Les Contamines. We had stocked up on hill food and snacks and it was the last place we could buy food for the day – the last shop before Courmayeur, around twenty-five miles away. One of the great things about the mountain huts in the Alps is how they manage to rustle up wonderful three-course meals in the evenings that are both filling and delicious and there's always lots of food for breakfast too. This meant we only needed to buy snacks for the daytime. While I run I eat little and often – never getting too full to make running uncomfortable while at the same time always looking to keep my energy levels topped up.

Les Contamines is a small village lying about halfway up its namesake valley. The valley itself is narrow, on its south-eastern side is the Mont Blanc massif and to the north-west a ridge leading to the triangular peak of Mont Joly. Given the valley's closed nature the town of Les Contamines is relatively quiet. After stopping at a supermarket and patisserie we sat down in the market square. I ate half a ham and reblochon tart I had brought at the bakery. Hardly the food of an athlete, but very tasty. I followed that with a few apricots while Andrea ate an apple and a pain au raisin.

After leaving town the route continues to follow the river. For a mile or so we ran along flat tarmac, although we could see this was soon to change. The valley started to become narrower as we steadily got closer to the Col de Bonhomme. We reached the last car park in the valley at the roadhead, and here the trail immediately got steeper, becoming rockier, and started to feel more mountainous. Initially we climbed through pine forest, again heading up to higher alpine meadow.

After threatening since we'd started in Les Bossons that morning the rain finally started to fall. We pulled waterproofs from our packs and pressed on. It wasn't cold, just very wet. Typical heavy Alpine rain – the kind that soon starts seeping into you, rain jacket or otherwise. The forecast was for it to get better through the day and then for a high pressure to settle in. Up until then, over the past few weeks the weather had been unseasonably bad – cold and wet. We were keeping our fingers crossed that a fine weather window with our names on it would soon to appear.

We passed the Chalet de Nant Borrant after a few miles of leaving the road. This refuge had a café that looked dry and inviting but we carried on, still having a reasonable distance to cover to the Mottets hut. We were making progress. Despite the fact that we could not see the lines of the valley for the trees, it felt like the valley was still narrowing as we made our way towards its head.

Soon the climbing lessened a little. We left the tree-lined track, reaching flatter meadow with cows grazing – bells around their necks clanging away. I refilled my water bottles at a water trough in the meadow on the edge of the track, next to an old wooden bench on which sat three men next to three big rucksacks. They were in their late teens or thereabouts. Despite sitting there in sopping wet rain ponchos, trying to boil a kettle, they seemed happy despite their stove failing to light, smiling at me and greeting me warmly. We shared some banter – they questioned why I was drinking water clearly intended for cattle. The water looked fresh and clean to me. I filled my bottles from the hose that fed running water into the trough from a stream higher up the hillside. I suppose they were trying to get their stove going to boil this water, but I didn't think there would be much risk in drinking it untreated.

The rain began to ease off, the col was out of the cloud, much closer now. After a few kilometres of flatter running, we started climbing steeply again, up towards the next mountain refuge we would pass, the Chalet de la Balme.

Then the sun came out, completely changing the day. Our immediate surroundings started to steam as the sun warmed the wet ground; we were glad to take off our waterproofs and stopped to put on some sunscreen next to the Chalet de la Balme. This hut is at 1,775m, set in a small corrie formed by the steeper ground up to the Col du Bonhomme and the mountaintops lying on either side of it. I had remembered this place from the first time I ran around the TMB. It was especially scenic and high enough to feel remote; after starting the route in the Chamonix valley it was the first time my sense of place felt truly mountainous. Up to our right was a jagged ridgeline formed by the Aiguille de Roselette. Wispy grey cloud hung around the rocky teeth of the ridge. With the sun the colours of the land became richer. As it shone on the wet grass of the meadow in the corrie there were deeper, more varied greens that contrasted with the blue sky that was fleetingly above us and the grey-pink rock of the ridge in-between.

The Col de Bonhomme was not far from us by now, around two miles and 600m of climbing. After the Chalet de la Balme the path steepened some more, the valley narrowed further as we approached the col. If I am honest it began to feel like a wet day out in Snowdonia, somewhere like the Ogwen Valley, heading up into the Glyders. There was low cloud, wet boulders to scramble over, my waterproof hood zipped tight against my head made me feel a little isolated from the others also climbing up to the col. There were quite a number of walkers at this point – we figured we had caught up with groups doing the TMB who had started their day in Les Contamines. As we got higher the weather closed in again. It was not the heavy rain of earlier, but a damp drizzle; not all that bad really and there was no wind to speak of.

Andrea reached the col some time before me. When we climb we generally do so at our own pace. This works well in everything except mountain marathons. As the navigator in these races I attempt to steer her from behind, shouting when I think she is going offline, or following someone she shouldn't. She puts up with this from me quite admirably.

When I reached the col Andrea was deep in conversation with a runner from the US who was waiting for his partner to catch up. I had recently passed her; we had exchanged greetings and had a brief chat. Like us they were heading to the Mottets hut for the evening.

From the Col de Bonhomme you then traverse the mountainside, and have some further climbing to reach the day's highest point. Initially there's about two miles to the Col de Croix de Bonhomme and then onto the Col des Fours – as I have already mentioned, one of the high points of the whole of the TMB.

We encountered our first snow of the route just beyond the col – a big patch that had a well-trodden path going across – luckily there was no need for anything like crampons or walking poles. With the gain in height it had got colder. It was still claggy, with lots of damp drizzle – we put our waterproofs back on and carried on to the next col. With the rocky trails and damp conditions I was again reminded of wet mountain days back in the UK – we could have been anywhere. On my previous run, the trail we were running along had been somewhat different. It had been later in the day, which had been beautifully clear, and by then I was running hard to make it to the hut in time for the evening meal. Despite this focus I still remember the view from up here. The path runs high above the wonderful Beaufortain region, the road linking the towns of Bourg-Saint-Maurice and

Beaufortain – the Cormet de Roselend – was clear to see. And I'd ridden that road before, when riding the road cycling version of the Tour du Mont Blanc.

We reached the Col de Croix de Bonhomme, marked by a large cairn. There is a hut just below the col, and from what we could see of it through the mist it looked inviting – given its location it must be a brilliant place to spend the night. We didn't stop long at the col – with the clag and temperature as it was we moved on quickly. Despite a route marker pointing to the Col des Fours and a reasonably clear path on the ground, I took out my compass and made sure we were headed in the right direction.

There was snow on the ground, which increased as we approached the col – soggy snow. While this meant our feet got wet, it was safe to cross relatively steep ground. Even so, as we reached the col and crossed it, beginning to descend down into the Vallee de Glaciers, we were initially wary of the line we took. It didn't take long, though, for us to drop below the snow line and for the cloud to clear, giving us some fantastic views down into the valley and up ahead. At one point the summit of the Aiguille des Glaciers appeared, surrounded above and below by cloud, looking high and inspiring. We hoped this improving weather meant that the forecast we'd read back at Les Bossons was accurate, and that the ensuing days would be sunny and clear.

This was my first time at the Col des Fours. When I'd run the TMB before, I went the alternative route, dropping from the Col de Croix de Bonhomme to Les Chapieux and staying overnight at the Auberge de la Nova. This refuge is at the entrance to the Vallee des Glaciers, close to the road leading up to the Cormet de Roselend and Beaufortain from Bourg-Saint-Maurice. I have many strong memories of this refuge and the close-by campground.

I'd been back to the Vallee des Glaciers in the summer of 2009, when I camped for a night or two before starting and finishing a two-day ride around the road cycling version of the Tour du Mont Blanc. In 2010 I was there for my first run around the TMB, and I went again in September 2011 to do some hiking. That time I was five months pregnant and on a trip to the Savoie region of the Alps with Aidan. We revisited a number of my favourite places – the Vanoise National Park, the Courmet de Roselend, Col du Petit Saint Bernard, the Vallee de Glaciers and Chamonix. This particular visit to the Vallee de Glaciers was somewhat more sedate than my first – hiking while pregnant felt a world away from the MountainX Adventure Race back in July 2008.

The MountainX race is one of the toughest and most amazing races I have ever done. The event spent five days traversing the Savoie region on the western flank of Mont Blanc. Racing in teams of three, the format of the race each day was a long endurance stage combined with a shorter mountain trail race. During the day we would complete the long stage and in the evening the trail race. This was a new format for adventure races – typically teams race non-stop (but for the occasional very short sleep) over four to six days. As such the pace is relatively slow. In the MountainX, given that we had the time to sleep for around six hours every night, the pace of the whole event was fast.

The race contoured a flank of Mont Blanc – the Savoie region – stretching from Bourg-Saint-Maurice in the south-east to Morzine in the north-west. During the day each stage was different, mountaineering, mountain biking, canyoneering and rock climbing, white water canoeing and finally a long-distance running stage into the Chablis Alps from Morzine. In the evening we had the trail races, heading into the mountains from where we would then spend the night and start the following morning's activity. So much was packed into a week. It was a crazy time that seemed to pass in a blur. Focus passed from one thing, to another and then the next. Sleep was always welcome but sometimes a hard thing to do, buzzing as I was from the intensity of each activity, as well as being excited and nervous about what was to come the following day.

I raced the event in a women's team with New Zealander Anna Frost and Lake District-based Chez Frost. The race started with a prologue on a Monday evening, a 12km race starting in the middle of Bourg-Saint-Maurice. With steep climbing up the mountainside to the north of the town and a fast pace, it gave us a taste of what was coming at us through the week. After that stage, the race moved on, up to the Vallee de Glaciers, where we all camped for the night on the ground out the front of the Auberge de la Nova at Les Chapieux.

The following morning had a 4am start for the mountaineering stage. This initially went up the valley to the Robert Blanc refuge, higher up the mountain and at 2,750m just below the snow line. It then followed the Pointe des Lanchettes ridge to the summit of the Aiguille de Glaciers. At 3,818m, this mountain climb and its descent was a hard stage that took a significant amount of planning and preparation for the race organisers. The stage itself was a mix of mountain marathon and high-level mountaineering. We started out wearing trainers and, when we got up to the snow line, changed to big boots, crampons and used a lightweight ice axe.

The ridge formed a sharp rocky crest. As we followed the fixed rope along its edge over our left shoulders we could see Mont Blanc to our right the greener valleys and peaks of the Beaufortain region. I felt elated – does it get any better than this? The sun shone brightly down on us, as we followed the ridge we were steadily closing in on another women's team from the USA, mindful of where we were but still racing hard.
From the summit of the Aiguille de Glaciers we descended by traversing the mountain's glacier on its southern face, following a marked route across and down the mountain. It felt bizarre but exhilarating to race like this, moving as fast as we could, roped together, wearing our big boots, ice axes ready to brace if we slipped.

After descending off the glacier we further traversed the mountainside, visiting a race checkpoint at the Col de la Seigne. This col lies on the TMB, and forms a border between France and Italy. While at the time I had little time to think about it as I was so busy racing, I knew I would be back, to cross over the col and to explore some more, when not embroiled in the intensity of fast racing. Even then I remember wanting at another time to be able to take the opportunity to relax, to be able to fully let the beauty of the place seep into me.

It is only now as I write these words I realise the pull the place has had for me. While it is one of the beautiful regions of the Alps, to be frank there are many more so why does it have this attraction? I think it must be the memories of my adventures here – it's the kind of place that encourages them, and why, six years after my first visit, and with my beautiful little girl back at home, I was back once more.

CHAPTER
FIVE

The trail off the Col des Fours into the Vallee des Glaciers was at first mainly scree – loose rocks with something of a footpath heading down them. The mountains above and around us would occasionally make an appearance as the cloud surrounding them cleared; at one point we got sight of the summit of the Aiguille des Glaciers, cloud above and below its peak with a suggestion of blue sky behind. This felt promising. As we got lower the path became less rocky, more defined and easier going, it eventually began to follow a large stream that ran down the hillside to the Ville des Glaciers, a small settlement of houses about halfway up the valley, between the Auberge de la Nova and Refuge des Mottets. We crossed this stream at one point and collected some water. Upstream of us was a small waterfall that over time had gouged the crag it ran over into an intricate and beautiful rock formation. The water tinkled as it raced over the rough and broken rock, sparkling in the sunlight.

Following the stream down to the Ville des Glaciers and then taking the track up to the Mottets hut was a dogleg – two sides of a triangle. I suggested to Andrea that in true mountain-marathon style we should take a more direct line to the hut; there just looked to be grassy hillside between us and it. We did this and eventually found a large, steep-sided gorge in our way. Idiot – I should have paid more attention to the map. By the time we found ourselves on good running ground again, we knew it would have been far quicker to take the established route.

Despite my attempts to make us late, we reached the hut with enough time to grab a shower and change before dinner. There were lots of people already there, many of them sorting out their kit in the large square space between the main building and the converted barns that were now dormitories and smaller bedrooms. The Refuge des Mottets was restored from an old farm and opened in 2010. There is a welcoming simplicity to it; the farmhouse itself now forms the communal eating area, the other buildings house basic accommodation that perfectly suited our needs for a warm and comfortable night's stay. On that first day we had covered around twenty-five miles. My body knew all about it, so I was looking forward to getting my head down.

Before that, however, came the evening meal in the hut. It was everything I hoped it would be – a veritable feast washed down with a beer, surrounded by people enjoying their time away in the mountains as much as me. The atmosphere was warm and cheery. Andrea and I got talking with the others sat around our large table; we shared our day's adventures and excitedly discussed those that were to come. It felt like all of us were happy to be in such a wonderful place. Many of us would be very weary after a long day, but that did not stop the beer and wine flowing along with good conversation.

Soon after the meal was finished we headed for bed. Instead of the communal dormitories we had each paid a few more euros for a room for four. We shared this with a Slovenian couple who were also doing the TMB. They were heading clockwise around the route, taking it steady due to what looked to be a very sore injury, given Ivan's pronounced limp and reliance on walking poles for support. Our room had two bunk beds, a few places to hang kit and that was pretty much it. It was all we needed. We both slept soundly until it began to get light the following morning.

Dawn broke to reveal a very different day from the one before. I opened the shutters and looked out the window to see a perfect deep blue sky and a wonderful view up to the Aiguille des Glaciers. The weather forecast had been correct – it was much improved, and we were excited about what that meant for the day ahead. The whole of the TMB is very scenic, but the route over and beyond the Col de la Seigne and down to Courmayeur is one of the most stunning sections.

Breakfast is always served early in mountain huts. Tea, coffee, cereal, bread and jam – we ate well and plenty. I drank a bottle of electrolyte alongside my hot drinks and felt a lot more hydrated. On long mountain days like these it doesn't pay to start the day feeling thirsty. We each carried a couple of tubes of electrolyte tablets that could be added to water. These are invaluable – water keeps you hydrated, of course, but it can also wash out too many of the minerals required by the body to function normally, initially leading to bad muscle cramps and then worse. Over the years I have suffered really bad cramps when racing – these pretty much stopped when I started using electrolyte tabs and now always carry a tube of them in a pocket when out for long days in the hills.

It was a chilly morning, waiting for the sun to reach the valley floor and warm the air but the day had all the makings of being a good one. We'd soon packed our kit and were ready to set off up to the Col de la Seigne. Some of those staying at the hut had started before us; others looked to just about ready be on their way.

So I was leaving this wonderful valley again, this time in the throes of another adventure. I keep coming back and I am sure I will again and again. Perhaps next time it will be with Alanna, to watch the marmots I saw close to the Refuge de la Mottets. The previous evening there were so many of them running around in the sun, calling to each other with their high-pitched whistles. I know she would be captivated by them.

On leaving the refuge there was not much chance to gently warm up weary legs. The climb was immediately steep – zigzagging up the hillside. This was one of those pronounced 600m or so climbs that the TMB seems to specialise in. Like leaving the Chalet de Bonhomme the day before, as we left the valley the climbing changed from a steady climb almost along the valley floor to following the line of least resistance up to the lowest point between us and the next valley.

As you cross the Col de la Seigne, leaving France and arriving in Italy, the scenery is sublime. My first sight of this valley was as memorable as it was brief. When Anna, Chez and I had approached this col during the mountaineering section of the MountainX, my mind had no real time to appreciate what I was looking at. I was too busy focusing on the map in my hand and the route we needed to take as we raced and could only steal a quick glance. Although not truly conscious of it then, the beauty had sunk in and in the ensuing months and years I found myself remembering the col, eventually indulging the growing urge to return by taking a plane to Geneva for a solo run around the TMB, when, without that intensity of racing I could properly see the mountains.

Racing is very intense, or at least it can be. Sometimes the winning can feel easy; other times so hard, so desperate. Chez and I first met at the Helvellyn triathlon in 2007, the year I won this race. In the previous two years I had finished second – that year I was quite determined to go better.

The Helvellyn triathlon is a great test of all-round fitness and speed. Set in the eastern Lake District, it takes in a 2km swim in Ullswater lake, a hilly 42-mile ride around the Helvellyn range and then a 9-mile fell run up and down Helvellyn. When I first heard about this race it seemed a perfect test of Lakeland mountain racing. These days there are a fair number of harder mountain triathlons in the UK nowadays, but at the time it was probably the toughest. The prospect of racing it was really exciting.

In 2005 I did this race as my first triathlon. I have not done all that many triathlons since, but I have always found the starts crazy. Wild thrashing in deep water as everyone tries to get a line through strong bodies all trying to do the same thing. By 2007, at the race start in Ullswater, I had learned from racing the event two years before that to stay calm, maintain a steady breathing pattern and to swim as smoothly as possible was the most important thing. Doing otherwise would mean going into the red – trashing yourself far too early in the race to be able to recover from quickly.

Often during races, after being in the lead or close to it and either dropping off the pace or being passed by a few other women, I would resign myself to finishing lower down the field. This time I didn't.

As ever with triathlons, I left the water in at least tenth place – I would have to catch up on the bike and likely continue to have to do so on the run up Helvellyn. After swimming the 2km loop in Ullswater, I ran out of the water to my bike in transition, peeled off my wetsuit, strapped up my cycle shoes and was soon back on more familiar ground – riding my road bike.

The effort I made cycling along the road by Ullswater warmed up my wet and dripping body and would eventually dry my clothes out a little. The bike leg of the triathlon took in a 40 or so mile loop around the Helvellyn massif, culminating in a tough climb up The Struggle out of Ambleside to the Kirkstone Pass before a fast descent back into Patterdale for the next transition.

I rode as fast as I could, counting down the women I passed among the men. I didn't know how many were ahead, I just wanted to pass them all.

Riding around to St Johns in the Vale from Threlkeld is where I first met Chez. She was riding in her now familiar style. We briefly chatted, introducing ourselves and then knuckled down to the racing. We figured we were placed about fourth and fifth women. Riding closely to each other over Dunmail Raise and past Grasmere, she got away from me on The Struggle. As I ground my way up this climb's steep hairpins towards the top I decided that this time I wasn't going to resign myself to second place again – I was going to win today.

The descent from the Kirkstone Pass is steep and fast, with a few bends that can throw out your line if you're not careful. A late Sunday morning on a perfect September day, the road was busy with tourists, cars and one big oncoming bus. I squeezed through a small gap between the bus and a car as we passed. That seems really stupid now. At the time I just wanted to keep my speed.

As I approached the second race transition I changed to an easier gear on my bike to spin my legs out and try to get rid of some lactic acid, drank from my bottle and ate half an energy bar, trying to best prepare myself for the last leg – the run up and down Helvellyn. On reaching transition I changed quickly into my running shoes and was off. Over the tannoy I heard that I was fifth woman, another four were ahead of me somewhere up the mountain.

From Glenridding the run up Helvellyn starts off pretty flat. Up the road, past the campsite until the first climb proper, up to Hole in the Wall. I remember thoughts coming into my head about work from earlier in the week. It had been a pretty tough one and my Chief Exec had to get involved with some of the things I was working on. Never a good sign – it had got pretty stressful. I consciously pushed those thoughts out of my head. I could not think of anything, just focus on the race.

Just before Hole in the Wall, at the bottom end of Striding Edge, I passed another woman. Fourth. I pushed harder as the race line crossed the corrie floor, passing Red Tarn and heading towards Swirral Edge. My legs were beginning to feel it by then. I ate a couple of jelly babies, took a gulp of water from the stream and continued on the climb up Swirral.

The path roughened and steepened towards the top. By then I was passing a lot of other racers who were running out of steam or perhaps out of their comfort zones. That is one of the things about the Helvellyn triathlon – it requires strength at many different disciplines – swimming, flat, steep and descending when cycling, steep mountain climbing and descending. All this and endurance too – it exposes your weaknesses.

I reached the top of the mountain and turned north, running again as best I could. A light mist made it feel a bit other-worldly. I passed another racer – a man. He encouraged me, telling me I was third woman; the other two were not far ahead, I should go for it. I pulled out an energy gel I had in my bumbag and squeezed it down, following it with the little water I had with me. That was that for food and drink until the end – now I had to nail it.

Off down the mountain, on the zigzags into Keppel Cove I soon passed the second placed woman. Now I was second, but where was Chez? I ran and ran, chasing and chasing – by this time there was no going back, no resigning myself to second again, I was going to win.

I didn't see her until I passed the Youth Hostel, on the track into Glen Ridding, about a mile from the finish. Steadily reeling her in, I had the advantage of knowing where she was in relation to me. She had not looked behind – showing her own strength of character – but I had a kind of upper hand.

I finally caught her, coming into the village, less than half a mile from the finish, as the track turned to road. And that was it, I cramped – Chez sped off. My legs seized and for a few moments I slowed to walking pace. It was very painful, but I managed to get running again after what seemed like an age. At the last corner of the race I caught her again. This time a shout came from me 'Come on!'. It was guttural, a groan more than a shout. I went and sprinted, finished the race in first place and promptly fell over just after the line.

I had never been so determined to win a race. I had started from behind and just kept at it throughout, steadily working myself up the field. To do it had required such a strong focus and such a big last effort. I was really pleased to win it. Proud I suppose, I knew the effort it had taken.

The pleasure of winning never really lasted that long, and what followed was a kind of downer from which escaping required another fix: I would set my sights on the next challenge. At the time, September 2007, my next challenge was the Three Peaks Cyclo-Cross. I had ridden this race six times, been second four times but had never won it and was even more determined to win this one. After Helvellyn that year I was worried that I had burned myself a bit, at least for a while. It had been an emotionally draining thing to do and I worried that I would not be able to psyche myself up. To run and race meant enjoyment often got obscured by the pressure I put on myself to win. After all, the win was what mattered…

In the grand scheme of things it was not a major win, but the triathlon in 2007 showed me what I could achieve if I really set my mind to it. Chez should really have won that race; she was the better athlete, I just wanted it more than her. I never beat her again after that, she got her own back and won the following year. I was back to second again.

In racing before and since Helvellyn I have never taken my head to where it was that day. It was so intense, in some ways it scared me. I don't remember anything else of the second half of the race apart from the robotic detail of what I physically needed to do to win. And robotic is a good description for it. There was no emotion, no pleasure in anything for me – not the mountains, the aesthetic of riding a bike, the fun in running down a fell side – just the focus and unblinking determination to win.

More recently I helped one of my friends, Derek, on his Bob Graham Round – the 65-mile, 24-hour challenge that covers 42 Lake District fells, climbing over 8,000m along the way. I helped him on the fourth leg, starting in the Wasdale valley and finishing by the slate mines at the Honister Pass. Derek had started running to a twenty-two hour schedule, but was going faster. Despite a low point during the long third leg through the Langdales and over the Scafells, by the time he got to Wasdale he was on for a sub-twenty-one hour round. During the leg I supported him on he got faster and faster, realising that he was feeling good and a sub-twenty was possible. He was right. He finished in nineteen hours and forty-five minutes.

It was fantastic to help him that day. I spent most of my time making sure he had enough to eat and drink, running slightly ahead to get the best line I could around the fells. At one point I turned and saw the look on his face as he ran from Pillar towards Kirk Fell. It was a look of nothing. Just an incredible, relaxed focus on what he was going to do that day. And what he did was quite something; he knew what he needed to do and got on with it. He achieved something brilliant that day and it was amazing to be able to help him. So this kind of robotic determination can help you to achieve great things. I think my problem was that this kind of achievement had become my only real goal.

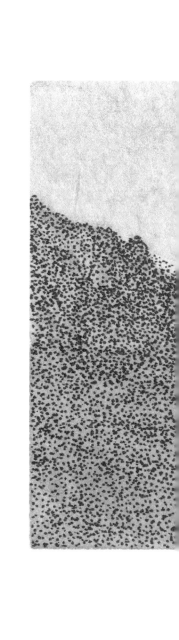

CHAPTER
SIX

In the early spring before I'd even started to plan this trip with Andrea I had flu, which stopped me doing any kind of training or racing for some time. Ironically it started during the first night of a family holiday to the Cairngorms at Easter – I spent most of a lovely spring week dozing on the sofa, recovering enough by the end of the week to take some short strolls with Alanna. During the ensuing weeks I recovered slowly from the virus but picked up a secondary chest infection, which left me feeling at least as bad. After the best part of three months coughing and spluttering whenever I ran or cycled, it wasn't until I headed out on this trip that I was finally beginning to feel like my normal self. I can't complain all that much – it had been my first real bout of sickness in around ten years. My legs, however, were complaining at the start of that second day – the first day was the first time I'd run any proper mountain descents for a long time – my muscles were sore, not really from fatigue, but from the pounding they had already received. When your body is accustomed to mountain running, this pain is a minimal thing. It was kind of a shock to feel like this again, almost like I needed to start over.

If my body was complaining, my mind was not – I was so thankful to be back in the Vallee de Glaciers. I love the view of the Aiguille de Glaciers from the Mottet hut – the memories I have of climbing this mountain during the MountainX race with Anna and Chez makes the place seem all the richer for me. I looked up to the mountain and remembered the efforts I had gone to. I had suffered with the altitude pretty badly towards the summit, recovering steadily as we ran as quick as we could down the glacier. Both Anna and Chez were faster than me, and I worked so hard to try to keep up, to not let myself and them down. It was hard work, a very tough day. Now, however, when I recall days like these, I don't really remember the feelings of pain or fatigue, just memories of racing hard surrounded by mountains.

The initial zigzag path up to the Col de la Seigne changed to a rising contour line as the gradient eased. The sun had risen over the horizon in our immediate direction of travel; it was warming and dazzling. The hillside changed in the sunlight – its colours and shadow lines enhanced by the brightness of the morning. I breathed it all in and knew then that these memories would come flooding back at some later point when I found myself painting and writing about this climb.

As with the day before on the Col de Bonhomme, Andrea gradually pulled away from me as we approached the col. I could see her up ahead and figured she was enjoying herself as much as me – this moment and all the other times she has been over this col. Her memories of the Mont Blanc massif are as vivid and lasting as my own. She first visited the Chamonix valley over twenty-five years before and like me has kept on coming back. Over the years she has climbed Mont Blanc twice, done the TMB three times and many other tours and long runs. In 2007 she was second in the Mont Blanc trail marathon, despite having suffered with a debilitating cramp during the last hour and a half of the race. She is tough and determined as well as a great and kind friend. We enjoy the time we spend in the hills together, generally talking about anything and everything. A month or so before we headed out to run around the TMB she found she had her PhD thesis accepted. That was some achievement as she combined her research with busy jobs as a social worker and university lecturer. She had aspirations for what she would do next academically, but at this point in time was taking some time to relax and enjoy the fact that she had the PhD in the bag.

The col got closer. Wide and shallow in nature, the gradient eased right off and the going got faster. When we reached the col we stopped for a while. All around us was a panorama we both remembered and were so happy to see again. The marmots seemed braver this side of the pass. We heard numerous whistles and got close enough to some that we could have touched them if we'd tried. Down the Vallon de la Lex Blanche valley, we could see the imposing knife-edge jagged rock ridges descending from the summit of Les Pyramides Calcaires. Opposite them on the other side of the valley the ridgeline formed by Mont Léchaud, Mont Pérce and Mont Fortin tempered the scene with its less domineering shape.

The path descending the valley formed a grey ribbon, twisting gently around and about to the left of the river. After a few miles the path passes below the Elisabetta hut, itself situated in a wonderful spot below the Glacier d'Estellette. Given the beauty and tranquillity of its location we had both really wanted to stay here, but it didn't fit into our four-day plan starting as we did in the Chamonix valley. Instead we stopped for a short while to rest and eat, enjoying the peaceful morning and the sun.

After the Elisabetta we descended the side of a rocky hairpin track. Here the valley flattened. The first time I did the TMB, having not looked at the map all that well, I had figured that it would be downhill from here all the way to Courmayeur. The climb up to a high point on the side of Mont

Favre was, therefore, a bit of a rude awakening. Another roughly 600m climb, this one crossed a shoulder of the mountainside over from the Val Vèny valley, taking a more direct route to Courmayeur than following the Val Vèny itself. This time I knew the climb was coming, I got on with it, remembering the views from the top of the pass. They more than recompensed the effort.

I also remembered the sight of the path descending from the high point down to the treeline and the next refugio at the Col Chécrouit. It was a long descending traverse that even my moaning legs would not complain about too much. Before we left the col we looked ahead, across the valley in which lay Courmayeur, to the Mont de la Saxe ridge and the summit of the Tête de la Tronche. This formed the alternate – higher route – of the TMB that we would take later in the day. When I had previously run the TMB I had stuck to the lower route. We were both keen – Andrea in particular – to do the higher routes this time around. With more climbing they were a tougher option but their location and the scenery afforded from them made doing them a bit of a no-brainer as long as we had the time. Andrea was full of enthusiasm for the stretch along the Mont de la Saxe and was also very much looking forward to the Fenêtre d'Arpette, a high col that would come later in our run the following day, shortly before we reached its finish at the Col de la Forclaz.

As a peak, the Tête de la Tronche is dwarfed by its surrounding neighbours – at 2,584m, despite being almost twice the height of Ben Nevis it seems more like a Scottish Munro than an Alp. Size doesn't always matter, however, and reaching a summit on the TMB rather than a mountain pass is a rare event. From where I was standing, the mountain looked like it had an audience with its surrounding peaks rather than being ignored by them with casual indifference.

We headed down towards the next hut where we planned to stop for a coffee and some food. The path we ran along continued to contour the mountainside, giving a feeling of shape and dimension to the terrain we were running over. I have a fascination with maps, and the ways in which they help me to interpret the ground I am travelling over is one of the reasons why. Their geometric nature is certainly another, appealing to the mathematical parts of my mind. There are times when I am running in the mountains when my head seems to click into a kind of 'abstract zone'. I become incredibly aware of the shape and nature of the terrain above, around and below me and the direction I am moving across it. If I am running holding a map in my hand, interpreting it as I run, it helps me to solve the immediate problem of navigating to where I am heading. In difficult conditions such as poor weather or darkness this can become incredibly absorbing, the focus required to find the way can be intense. As I ran down the mountainside towards the refuge along a wide clear path in the sunshine, none of this focus was required. It was absorbing nonetheless – yet another way to see and feel the mountains, and one that it is very important to me.

Map reading and navigation are skills that have taken me years to get to grips with. While I am much better at them than I was, I still make plenty of mistakes. I love the way I have to think and run at the same time, to interpret the contours of the map to form 3-D mountains in my head and then to translate these mind images to the world around me.

Thinking for myself in this way, and more generally, is something that is becoming increasingly important to me. A substantial part of my consultancy work involves analysing data, using statistical and computational methods and processes that over time help machines to become ever more able to essentially 'think' for themselves. Artificial intelligence is one of the great developments of our time and perhaps one of the most dangerous.

Since the beginning of the industrial revolution, we have continually handed over more and more of our labour to machines. This started with the manual tasks and has increasingly moved into tasks that require less motion and arguably a greater capacity to think and make decisions. Global Positioning Systems are a key example of this. I do not like them. It may sound paranoid, but we need to be mindful of what we are giving away when we use machines to do our thinking for us. As a society we are steadily losing the capacity to think for ourselves, becoming lazier – more stupid? We should be valuing our capacity to be creative far more, encouraging and nurturing thinking for ourselves, rather than giving it away to a machine. It is our appreciation of beauty and capacity to be creative that keeps us different from machines. Until the technical development of artificial intelligence solves what perhaps will be its last great problem – that to be human means that we can be irrational as well as rational in our thinking, original as well as logical – (the so-called Lovelace test) – this difference will remain.

And here we come to what I think is a great paradox of racing around mountains. In doing so we may be pushing ourselves to be our absolute physical best, but to get the best out of yourself when doing so you need to be robotic. An automaton. To focus entirely on the task in hand, and what you need to do to go the fastest you can go. Anything else – daydreams, conversation with friends, appreciation of the scenery, allowing your mind to wander – perhaps solving problems in another area of your life – coming up with the next painting, written work or solution to that challenging piece of software design – has to go by the wayside. Racing can be amazingly absorbing, a wonderful thing in itself. But I find going to the mountains one of the very best places to think. While I love pushing myself hard physically, I don't think I can force myself to stop thinking any more.

As we descended towards the col we hit the treeline. There were more people here – out walking from the top of the chair lift from the valley. We were around 700m above the Aosta Valley floor and Courmayeur, and would follow the route of the chair lift for some of our descent down into town. We sat outside the refuge and drank coffee. I had also had a coke,

Looking back towards the Elisabetta Hut

some chocolate cake and half a large cheese and ham panini (I wrapped the other half in a napkin for later). Andrea had a coffee and the other half of the pain au raisin she had been carrying since our breakfast the previous morning in Les Houches. Whenever we are out for long days she stows away either fruit scones or pastries of some description, bringing them out at opportune moments to enjoy.

It was around midday. We had probably gone around twelve miles since leaving the Mottets hut and had about twenty miles to go to where we planned to spend the night in the Elena Refugio. This hut sits across the valley from the Glacier de Pré de Bar and directly below the Grand Col Ferret – the Italian-Swiss border. Each day's mileage was an estimation for us; going on past experience and given that we needed to complete the route in four days, we roughly planned each day based upon approximate distance. Three longer days of between twenty-five to thirty miles, and then a shorter final day from the Col de la Forclaz through to Chamonix.

As well as a greater distance, the latter half of our day would have more climbing. We figured if we kept to the same steadyish pace we would reach the Elena in time for a shower before dinner. This also meant we couldn't linger too long over our lunch – a shame as sitting outside in the sun felt good.

We left the alpine meadow we'd been relaxing in and followed a line down through the pine forest for the four miles down to Courmayeur. The path zigzagged steeply down the mountainside and through the trees – typical of lower alpine trails, with a smell of pine and dappled light that I will forever in my mind link to running and biking adventures in the Alps.

By now my legs were giving me a fair bit of pain descending. Nowadays there is an established scientific term for it – Delayed Onset Muscle Soreness – the dreaded DOMS. Before this establishment, fell runners in the UK, and in particular Scottish hill runners had the term – 'Ben legs' – referring to the soreness that hits the legs a day or so after the annual Ben Nevis race. The 1,300m descent off Ben Nevis is particularly tough – rocky and fast – leading to sore legs for even the most seasoned fell runners. Unless they become chronically bad, sore legs caused by lots of descending are not something that would threaten me finishing the TMB. I made of point of massaging them whenever I could which helped, but they did slow me down, making our long day a little longer.

The air became hotter and hotter as we descended. In the trees we had some shelter from the sun, which seemed to be trying to make up for lost time after the previous day's cloud and rain. After many zigs and zags in the trail we popped out of the trees onto tarmac and had a mile or so to go before central Courmayeur.

CHAPTER
SEVEN

'There is no substance but light'

Nan Shepherd, 'Embodiment', *In the Cairngorms*

This was my second visit to Courmayeur. Much like the first time I would only be passing through. As with Les Contamines the day before, this was a shame as Courmayeur felt like the kind of place where I could stay for a long time. This is not surprising. Given its position at the foot of the Italian side of Monte Bianco, Courmayeur has a place in the history of Alpine mountaineering, skiing and all other kinds of mountain-going to rival Chamonix.

The route of the TMB passes through the narrow alleyways of the village of Dolonne before you cross over the river and reach the centre of Courmayeur itself. It felt refreshing to walk along the shaded streets, sheltered from the heat of the sun by the shadows cast on the narrow streets of terraced homes and other dwellings.

Deep pink flowers contrasted with the dark brown and creams of the buildings, the blue of the sky and the greens, browns, greys and dazzling white of the mountains and their tops. This part of the town felt like it had not changed for a hundred years or more. There was a palpable sense of history that got me thinking about the past residents – who were they, what adventures did they have in the mountains?

From Courmayeur we would climb again, out of the Aosta valley, back up into the hills surrounding the massif. The route climbs steeply up to the Bertone hut, from here continuing along the Mont de la Saxe to the summit of the Tête de la Tronche. After this we would descend into the Val Ferret, passing the Bonatti hut to finish our day at the Elena hut and the foot of the Grand Col Ferret, the Italian-Swiss border.

I had been really looking forward to this section and had enjoyed it so much the last time. While space was limited in my rucksack for this trip, I had allowed myself the luxury of a book, and like the first time I ran the TMB, it was Walter Bonatti's *The Mountains of My Life*. Perhaps this shows I am a creature of habit but it is such a great book, one I keep coming back to. I wanted to feel the same inspiration I had felt the last time – to travel his paths, look up to his mountains, read his words and marvel at the combination of them all.

A long-time resident of Courmayeur, Bonatti was one of those I had in mind when passing through the old town. *The Mountains of My Life* is his account of his development and achievements as a mountaineer – from his time as a boy walking in the foothills of the Alps in northern Italy, to becoming one of the foremost climbers of all time. It is inspiring to read of all of his achievements, but also to read of how he achieved them. He did them all with his own sense of ethics and values that would have made them harder, but also more honest and pure. Travelling along the paths he traversed, looking up to the massif and the tenacious lines that he climbed first, and often solo, filled me with awe. His was a fearsome drive, tremendous courage, a real vision for a climbing line and a sense of the aesthetic, all the time keeping to a set of values. Given that at the time these were some of the hardest routes ever climbed, his achievements stand out all the more.

Each time I have read it, his book has drawn me in with both his tales of how he climbed the routes he did and how he did so following his own rules. He found it hard to climb or simply to be with people who either did not share or sympathise with these values. As such, he did not make things easy for himself in either his climbing or his relationships. He must have been stubborn as hell and often hard to relate to, but you get the sense that those people he considered friends received the utmost kindness and loyalty from him.

Bonatti did his last major climb in 1965 when he was thirty-five – a solo ascent of the North Face of the Matterhorn. After that he still climbed and spent much of his time in the mountains, but his focus shifted from climbing the most challenging of routes in wild mountain environments to travelling around them, capturing them in photography and writing. There is a theme of wilderness and journeying to his work. He still clearly needed to suffer in wild and remote places, but his focus shifted from audacious mountaineering to a more detailed appreciation of the sense of beauty of the places he travelled to and through.

I could, of course, never say for sure, but maybe, when Bonatti retired from cutting-edge mountaineering and moved on to wilderness exploration and photography, he also found that the way he perceived mountains changed and grew. His creative abilities extended beyond his achievements as a mountaineer; in his photojournalism trips to some of the world's wild remote places for the magazine *Epoca*, some of his other talents shine through.

An innovator in many ways, some of the lines he first climbed took tremendous ingenuity and self-belief – he was pushing everything: his body, mind, equipment, technique and his friendships. He continually experienced the disbelief and even contempt of others – stuck as they were within their personal limits and likely envious of Bonatti as he strove to stretch and exceed his own. Likewise, his individualism shines through in his writing and photography; you sense that he wrote to explore himself as much as he wanted to explain himself to others.

To say I found inspiration in the honest and beautiful writing of one of the world's greatest ever mountaineers is perhaps an obvious thing. For me though, it went further than just gaining inspiration to the extent of empathy I felt with him. I don't think I mean that I wholly understand the places he went to both physically and mentally when he was climbing the routes he did – I can only imagine that, and do so with awe. What I mean is that I empathised with his desire to change and move on. When in his thirties he chose to turn his back on hard new routes he did not stop climbing in the mountains, but changed his focus to different challenges. I had spent years racing and racing, never stopping to think and look at the world around me in other ways. Reading Bonatti's words encouraged me to be brave, to push some other limits and see what I could further find in myself. I am grateful for that.

Looking back I think *The Mountains of My Life* (and, therefore, Bonatti) has helped me to open my mind up to the idea that I should paint mountains as well as run and cycle up them. When I think about it now there had kind of been a little voice in the back of my head for years, encouraging me to lose some of my inhibitions, forget about the training and racing a little, to express myself in a different way. Reading Bonatti's book and spending some time in his mountains, not racing but travelling, helped me to listen to that voice, to get hold of an easel, canvases and paints, to shake away at least some of my reserve and begin to paint. I honestly think that this is one of the best things I have ever done – though it has nothing to do with however skilled I might be. The interpretation of art is a subjective thing, the process of its associated creativity all-encompassing, absorbing and relaxing. I can lose myself in a painting just as much as I can running up a mountainside.

I experience creativity in my painting, writing and in the real-world application of mathematical theory. These three things are quite diverse, but in doing each of them I get my head to the same place. It is an exciting and stimulating place and, perhaps surprisingly given that, a place that calms and even soothes me. When I feel stressed, a little painting, writing or (dare I say it) mathematical problem-solving time can do me the power of good. Much like going for run or a bike ride.

More than that, painting mountains has helped me to see them in a different way. I always appreciated their stature and beauty but now I look at them differently, almost with a more enhanced sight. I also now understand what it means when there is 'good light'. When I am out running or cycling and see it, I can't help but comment to my companions – though I don't know what they make of that.

When I spend time out in the mountains now I always carry my camera, even when I am racing. I learnt a lesson in August 2014, while running the Sedbergh Hills fell race in the Howgills. These hills are some of my very favourites to run in, they lend themselves so well to it, wonderful smooth ridges so well defined and interlinked, which all the time feel remote and quiet.

I was having a bad race; my legs felt heavy, and I generally had no zip. A few miles into the route, contouring the fell side north towards the Black Force waterfall, I resolved to just chill out and enjoy my time in the hills, running along at a pace I could maintain without feeling too bad. A late summer's day out on the fells of Westmorland with sunshine and cloud and a breeze to keep me cool while running. Perfect conditions – it couldn't get much better.

One scene from this race has stayed in my mind – it was when I looked up the valley formed by Langdale Beck, as I climbed out heading east. The clouds and sun combined to create the beautiful dappled light typical of the Dales in summer. This light brought out wonderful colours on the fell side – golden greens, yellows and browns, along with shadows that defined the ripples and lines of the valley with a great deal of depth. I remember feeling so appreciative of this beauty and felt a strong desire to paint the scene in an attempt to capture the colours and the shape of the sky and the fell for my own posterity. I had no camera and couldn't record the moment. So frustrated that I'd missed this chance, I even went back the following weekend to try to capture the scene. The weather was different and so was the light – I will never see that valley in that way again.

Mountains never look the same way twice. The weather conditions, the season and the time of day combine to make them unique. Sometimes these combinations can be obviously jaw-dropping in their beauty, other times I find I need to take my time – to look a little longer. The beauty appears as I take the time to properly see, the associated thrill is a consuming thing. God it was good, that day in the Howgills. While it is not the end of the world that I didn't get a photograph from which I could paint, it is something I regret. I don't think it's necessary for me to capture and attempt to paint all the beautiful scenes I see when I am out and about in the hills, but sometimes the anticipation at what I could try to capture when painting mountains is at least as thrilling for me as the time I spend in the mountains themselves.

After my experience in the Howgills I wanted to explore the feelings I had some more, and to find others who understood them. In reading *Lakeland Portraits* by William Heaton Cooper – one of the finest painters of Lake District landscapes – I learned his own thoughts on looking at mountains.

> Sometimes I have looked at a mountain landscape, have been moved by its beauty and strength, yet have failed to realise it as being much more than a volume of rock, some solid and some broken, standing rather higher than its surroundings. Yet even as I looked the design gradually revealed itself and I could read the story of each fold and buttress, swelling roundness and shattered crag.

As well as establishing the Heaton Cooper gallery in Grasmere in the Lake District, painting a significant body of work and publishing several books, Heaton Cooper was a well-known Lakeland rock climber. Along with climbing bold routes he sketched and painted some of the guidebook route illustrations for the Fell and Rock Climbing Club. He carried a sketchbook with him when he went climbing and walking in the Lakes, sometimes painting entirely on location. His thoughts on how as a painter he looked at mountains were clear and down to earth.

> This simple act of seeing, too simple sometimes for clever or complicated people to grasp, and yet available to all, is the open secret of the painter. And it is here that every picture begins to be painted.

I think I discovered this secret in 2011 when I got hold of an easel, oils, a few brushes and some canvases and started to paint. My first painting was of Beinn an Eoin, one of the mountains of Flowerdale, north of Torridon and to the south-east of Gairloch in the Scottish Highlands. The first time I had laid eyes on Flowerdale was in November 2009 when Aidan and I were running Torridon's Beinn Eighe ridge. I was smitten. The mountains of the Flowerdale Forest rise up from the tundra that surrounds them. Bold, striking hills, with a sense of remoteness rare to find in the UK. I came back to Flowerdale in the spring of 2010, when Andrea and I ran around them during the Highlander Mountain Marathon. As we travelled back south after the race I took the photographs that over the next year would gently whisper to me to try painting them.

In reading Heaton Cooper's words I now feel an affinity with him – I don't know if I am ready to call myself an artist just yet, but I understand him, his passion for light and his understanding of the way he looked at mountains, and how light impacted on this. It feels like I am cheating a fair bit to carry a digital camera rather than a sketch book, but in photographing and then painting mountain scenes I aspire to capture light in the way Heaton Cooper did in his paintings. Many of his works are breathtaking in their simplicity and beauty. These days I know enough about painting to understand that, while it may appear simple, the ways in which Heaton Cooper gave the impression of the shape of a mountain or crag, light and stature with just a few brushstrokes was masterful. He looked at mountains and their rock faces as both a painter and a climber, which is why his work for the Lakeland rock-climbing guidebooks is both so beautiful and so useful. Being able to see with the eye of both these disciplines surely leads to an improved perception of the mountains altogether.

Descending to the Bonatti Hut

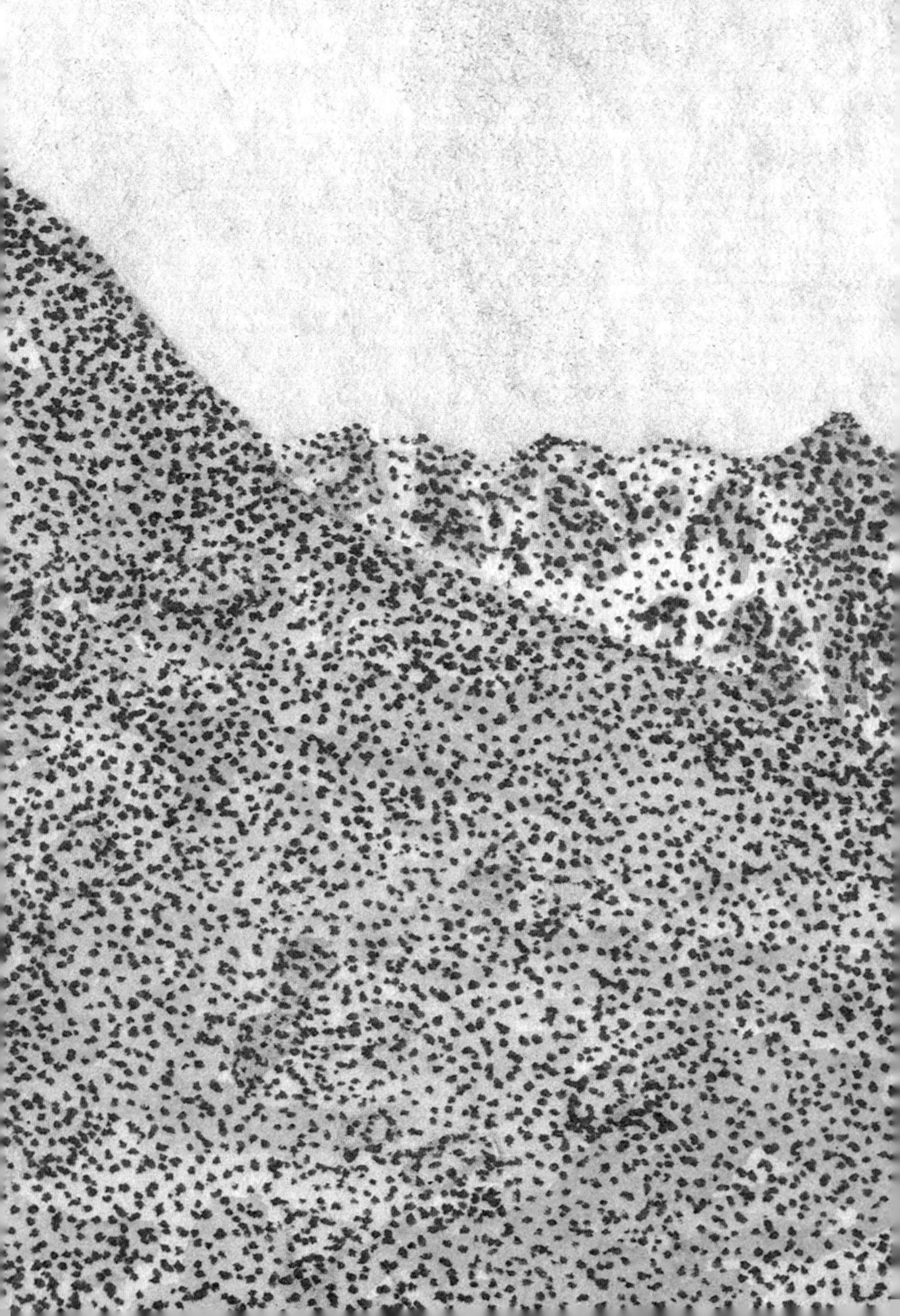

CHAPTER
EIGHT

And so to the climb out of Courmayeur. On fresh legs it would have been very enjoyable. Another zigzagging line up through pine trees that sheltered us from much of the afternoon's heat. While it was enjoyable, in all honesty I was looking forward to reaching the Bertone hut, as shortly after that the trail would steady off and the view would be superb, both of which would help to take my mind off my complaining legs. We still had a way to go to reach the Elena in time for dinner and we knew it. However, before that we also knew that coming up was one of the best panoramas the Tour du Mont Blanc has to offer. The Mont de la Saxe ridge offers unsurpassed views of the south-west face of the Mont Blanc massif and it really is enough to take your breath away.

A couple of mountain bikers descended the trail as we climbed and we passed a few other walkers as they moved up the hillside following the trail. While the TMB must be one of the most well-travelled routes in the Alps, it rarely actually felt busy. The climb continued and eventually the treeline became clear to see. While the day grew cooler, it was still hot as we ascended. I'd drunk nearly all my water and planned to refill my two bottles from the fountain outside the Bertone hut. Andrea was up ahead, climbing to her own pace. She was really looking forward to the next few miles; one of her favourite sections of the entire route.

As we left the trees we reached a corner of the trail with a particularly fine view of the Peuterey ridge. I declared that I was going to sit down for five minutes or so and finish off the second half of my stowed panini. I sat by the side of the path, gazing up to the Peuterey ridge and other beautiful features of the massif, and was once again awed by Bonatti's achievements in that environment. I have only been up high on the massif once, in my very early days of being a climber. I have strong memories of the place and the feelings evoked by being in it. If I had returned again and again and got to know these mountains far more than I actually do, I think the sense of mystery I harboured of the place when I was nineteen would probably have gone. In a way I am glad it is still there.

Refreshed by the short break and food, I got to my feet and we continued. We passed the Bertone refuge and I refilled my bottles. From here we had more climbing, but it steadied off after the first steep section up onto the Mont de la Saxe ridge. The route followed the ridge up to the summit of the Tête de la Tronche.

Mont Blanc from the Bertone Hut

The first time I ran around the TMB I had taken the lower route to the Bonatti from the Bertone. This followed a contour line that runs parallel to the Mont de la Saxe ridge, with less height and distance to the alternative we were taking. This ridge was, therefore, new to me, but not to Andrea. She had been speaking about its beauty since we'd met at the airport on Sunday evening, and she was not wrong. Green, grassy and smooth, the ridge felt like it would be at home in Snowdonia or the Lake District. Surrounded by Alpine giants, it felt a perfect balcony.

As we steadily climbed I ate some sweets. My body was beginning to feel even more tired and so I snacked a little more. I normally take days like these in my stride. I hoped that my increased fatigue was not a sign of general decline, but more a reflection of the fact that I had only just properly recovered from the worst bout of flu I'd had in ten years. While I'm not as bothered now about doing these kind of long days as fast as I can, I do want to be able to keep doing them. Other than the flu, there are other reasons for why I have slowed down. One is my age – I'm not getting any younger! Also, since becoming a mother, given that I now get far fewer days out in the mountains than I used to, I want to slow down, to value them and live in the moment, rather than spend the whole time looking at my feet trying to go as fast as I can from one place to the next.

The ridge curved to the right as we approached the summit. A small cairn marked its top. We stopped for a breather, to take in the view and have a look at the map. It was half past five. We figured we still had about 18km to go to the Elena. The Bonatti hut was closer, about 8km away. Given that we wanted to get a shower before the hut dinner at half past seven, we decided to see if we could instead stay at the Bonatti. Andrea pulled out her phone. A few minutes later she had phoned her husband Mark, who had promptly texted her the number of the Elena and the Bonatti. On booking two beds, dinner and breakfast at the Bonatti, she phoned and cancelled our booking at the Elena. All sorted from a mountaintop. While easy to do, it felt little like cheating.

From the top of Tête de la Tronche I'd been hoping that it would be all downhill to the Bonatti. We could see, however, that after our first descent into a high hanging valley, we would have another fifteen minute or so climb up to another col, after which we would descend to pop out of a little valley right above the Bonatti. I reconciled myself – only a little climb, and it looked a great line and not as far to go as we had originally planned before we could stop for the night.

The path from the summit initially descended down into what in Scotland would be called a corrie, and then contoured across rocky but runnable ground to the bottom of the climb up to the Pas Entre-Deux-Sauts col. Now early evening, the light was changing. There was still some time before the sun would drop behind the mountains, but it was lower in the sky and this was evident in the shadows and colours of the rocks and mountains. We again had the trail to ourselves – most other people walking today must have been either finished for the day, relaxing in their hut, tent or other rest stop, or taking the lower trail around the other side of the Mont de la Saxe. I remember running across the corrie and feeling a terrific sense of peace. This was countered in my head by a hustling urge to get on with it to make it to the hut in good time.

By now I had pretty much run out of food. I had packed in a couple of energy gels for such situations and squeezed one down – it was gloopy, its sugar-filled caffeine-perked coffee flavour tasted wholly artificial (funny that), but I felt its kick as I climbed and was thankful for it. We were definitely on the last leg now, just a few more miles until the Bonatti. There I would take off my shoes, sit down for a while, hopefully find a bag of crisps. After that I would find a bed in the *dortoir*, unpack my bag, have a shower and then dress for dinner. Dressing for dinner constituted putting on the T-shirt and shorts I had with me for the evenings. I ran in all the other clothes I had with me – by now they stank. On lightweight trips like these you pare things down, and take a great deal of pleasure at the end of the day in simple things like taking your shoes off.

When we reached the col, I was tired, and wasn't really that bothered about the fantastic location – I just wanted to get to the hut and stop for the day. We followed a good path that thankfully ran down a shallow valley. Soon we popped out above the much wider Ferret valley, immediately above the Bonatti. Our place for the night, and what a place it was.

Outside the refuge, lots of the evening's residents were sitting on benches and boulders, basking in the scenery and the last of the evening sun, which soon would sink below the mountain. What a wonderful situation – I think everyone must have realised this – there was a sense of happiness and satisfaction in the air. And I was wholly satisfied with our wonderful day in the mountains.

I took off my shoes. While thankfully I had no blisters or anything painful going on with my feet, it felt lovely to let them breathe in the open air. They were bearing up well, given the last two days. We checked in and I brought a bag of salted crisps from the bar. I joined all the others sitting in the sun, and ate my crisps, saying nothing, just gazing at the Mont Blanc massif directly across the valley from where we sat.

Looking down the valley to my left, on the horizon was the Col de la Seigne. The beautiful valley ahead of it burned bright with vivid colours in the evening light. I have such strong memories of just sitting and gazing at that scene, revelling in the place and the day's adventure. A journey along a mountainside, up, down and over valleys, past refuges and through old towns that themselves carry so many memories, histories of other people's adventures, and of their lives. Bonatti's choice of stomping ground is surely one of the best.

The sun eventually went down behind the mountain. It was not all that late, just that the mountains surrounding the Bonatti hut were close by and so much higher than the building itself. Most of us sitting outside the hut stayed put, carrying on with conversations, drinking coffee or a beer, generally relaxing. I went back into the hut to have a shower and sort out my kit before dinner. The water in the shower was warm. I washed away the day's accumulation of salt and grime.

I was soon ready to go to the large dining room and sit down for dinner. On our table that evening were two women from the US – Claire and her daughter Monica – who that day had started walking the TMB in Courmayeur. They had travelled to Europe as part of Monica's thirtieth birthday celebrations. Andrea and I spoke at length with both of them. Claire in particular felt rather daunted at what she had just started, wishing she had worked out more before heading over, and that she hadn't packed as much kit as her bag was heavy. Claire and Monica had enough time to take over twenty days doing the route if they needed. This meant they could fit rest days in too. We tried to reassure Claire with all of this. That she had got to the Bonatti from Courmayeur in a day boded well, and I think she knew that. I hope she got into it after a few days and realised that though it was a tough prospect, she could do it and enjoy her wonderful trip with her daughter all the more.

One of the great things about the TMB is its relative accessibility; anyone who is fit enough to walk eight miles or so a day for two weeks, taking in climbs along the way of around 600m, can do it. While I know that this puts all individuals who complete the TMB in a relatively small proportion of the population it is something that is achievable by many with some walking to build up to it beforehand. This accessibility does not detract from the achievement of completing it – 105 miles around the Mont Blanc massif requires tenacity, particularly if it is not something the body and mind is familiar with.

Dinner arrived. Three courses – soup, a rich stew with vegetables, followed by chocolate tart. Having washed it down with a couple of glasses of red wine, I left the table feeling full and tired. I had a quick look out of the door across the valley again and then headed to bed.

The Bonatti is a large mountain hut – it has around 80 beds. Like the Mottets hut the night before, we got a choice of accommodation, ranging from small rooms with two or three bunks to the large dormitories – *dortoirs* – that would sleep over 20 people. That night we were in the biggest dorm in the Bonatti, which could fit in 40 people when it was full. The beds were arranged on a single level, running against the walls of the large room. When sleeping next to someone you would be pretty close to them, so I hoped they didn't snore. I had stayed before at the Bonatti and slept in the same room as the first time I ran the TMB. The hut had been rammed then – all beds taken – and I ended up next to a man who looked to be staying there with two of his grandchildren. He snored loudly all night. Intermittently through the night I lay awake, silently cursing him, eventually wanting to hit him. Not too hard, just enough to get him to stop. Andrea and I were luckier this time – the *dortoir* was less than half full and we each had a little more space to ourselves.

The hut opened in 1998. Bonatti died in 2011, aged eighty-one. It forms a great tribute to him – in its perfect setting with photographs from his climbing and photojournalism days adorning the walls. As I walked to the dorm I stopped to look at them – there he was in Patagonia, paddling the Yukon, climbing on Mont Blanc. On going to bed I read a few more pages of his book before my eyes insisted I give in.

I slept well. All too soon it was morning and people began to stir just before 6am, getting up to ready themselves for the day ahead. I joined them, getting dressed, packing up my bag and heading along to the dining room for breakfast. After tea and coffee, juice, muesli and bread and jam I felt more awake and ready to go.

At around quarter to seven Andrea and I were again sitting outside the front of the hut with some others. It was another blue sky morning, the air was cool, the sun yet to rise, something it would do soon. As I put my shoes on I felt a real sense of anticipation for the day ahead.

Claire was outside too and we chatted some more about what was coming next – they were heading over the Col de Grand Ferret to La Fouly. We also spoke some more about each of our daughters. As mothers we were at different stages – Monica was thirty, Andrea's daughter eighteen and at university, and my daughter was then just two. We were all silent as the sun came up, watching it begin to light the mountainside we faced felt almost spiritual – the shared moment special.

Despite wanting to linger a little longer – part of me felt like I could gaze up at that mountainside forever – my bag was packed and we were all set to go. Our day would take us to the Col de la Forclaz. This is a road pass, close to the French-Swiss border and the Chamonix valley. There is a large hotel at the col that had a *dortoir* attached, and this is where we planned to stay that evening. Andrea and I had discussed our day's route the night before. From memory we decided that it was around twenty miles. Given our 7am start time, we were hoping that this would mean we would be sitting outside the hotel in the sun by early afternoon. Before then we had the Grand Col Ferret and Col de la Fenêtre to climb up to and cross. We would leave Italy and arrive in Switzerland, continuing on our journey around the Mont Blanc massif.

The path the TMB follows from the Bonatti up the Ferret valley gently contours the mountainside, very runnable, with views of the Triolet glacier and its surrounding mountains high above the other side of the valley. The air was still cool, our surroundings now brightened by the sun, a perfect setting for the beginning of our day's run.

Mont Blanc from the Bonatti Hut

CHAPTER
NINE

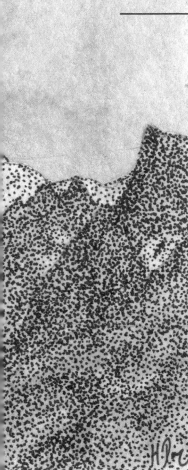

Whether climbing, cycling, running or all three, racing or making my own way, Alpine mornings have always felt special to me. The bright sunlight, white-topped mountains, cool air and sense of anticipation (often mixed with trepidation) of what the day ahead would bring has often formed the beginning of some of my toughest physical challenges, and most memorable mountain days. In doing multi-day challenges like the Transalp mountain bike race, MountainX race and Cent Cols Challenge, I always found I quickly got used to the routine of early morning starts. This routine is quite unlike that of 'normal' life; the focus soon becomes more basic – making sure you eat enough and that your body is still fit and able to deal with the stresses and strains of the day ahead. The night-time routine is trying to get enough sleep to ensure you are as fresh as you can be.

When not racing, I can still revert to this basic lifestyle and it gives me more time to think and more time to appreciate my surroundings. Much of this thinking is introspective and it has come to make me realise what racing was, at least in part, doing for me. It was stopping me from thinking. In turn, I have realised that at least part of the reason I did this was through a subconscious fear that I would end up like my dad. He used to sit, read and think about engineering for hours on end in his chair at home. As time passes, with reflection and a greater distance I have begun to appreciate what an impact this had on me. During the times he was at his most unwell, in seeing him mentally so lost, I associated his deep thinking with that state of mind. Of course there was a link – spending too much of your time gazing at formulae is not healthy – but there doesn't have to be. With this awareness has come a sense of release. I feel braver now.

In finding new confidence to explore myself intellectually and artistically I have also found that I have less of a drive to race. This is no doubt combined with the fact that I have a family to spend time with now, and less time to train and race. A bit of a chicken and egg situation – did I feel ready enough to become a mum because of this change in focus or did becoming a mum help me to change my focus? Whichever – it doesn't really matter, I'm glad it has all happened.

Nowadays I train when I can fit it in, with a main focus on enjoying it, clearing my head and trying to maintain a fitness to be able to do things like run around the Tour du Mont Blanc over a few days without suffering too much. My drive to achieve is still there, but I am directing it in other ways. In doing so I am learning so much, and combining this learning with other experiences to try out new things.

While mathematical modelling, statistical analysis and software development are very logical processes, they are similar to painting and creative writing in that innovation in them requires a large amount of creative thinking and intuition – as well as attention to detail and an understanding of the concepts underlying the application, an ability to problem solve and to visualise the overarching solution requires creative thinking. I am not sure you can learn how to do this kind of thinking. I think it's probably innate in most of us, but gets gradually eased out of us as we grow and are educated. Looking back on my own education I think that this happened (despite a pretty strong rebellion from me).

One of the things I always seem to push against is the pressure to conform. This has frequently made things much harder than they could be for me, but I have also achieved the most when shirking convention and doing things differently. If you conform, you think with the crowd and how then can new things happen? I can't help but ask questions – why like this, why not the other, why don't you do it this way?

Writing these words makes me smile, as I know where most of my 'why' questions are coming from these days – Alanna. Her mind is clear of clutter and like a sponge, her thinking and learning processes a joy to watch and be a part of. During the days I spent writing this chapter I also painted a map of Kintail and Glen Affric in the north-west Scottish Highlands. One afternoon Alanna declared she also wanted to paint. We sat together with brushes and watercolours, merrily splashing away. At one point Alanna looked at a section of what I was doing and told me I had painted a giraffe. While this was actually the topographic outline of the Five Sisters of Kintail (or at least that is what I hoped), she was completely right – looked at with a different eye, it did have similarities to a giraffe.

Young children are such free thinkers, brave and bold without even realising it, letting their imagination express itself unfettered from worry about what people will think of them for doing so. Generally we become more inhibited as we get older. I know I did. The author Philip Pullman helped me to realise that it was not just our education system that did this to me as I grew. In a preface written for a later publication of *His Dark Materials* trilogy, Pullman writes of the indebtedness the storyline has to Henrich Kleist, a little-known philosopher from the nineteenth century. In an essay entitled *On the Marionette Theatre*, Kleist discusses how as a child grows into adolescence and then adulthood, they become self-aware. With this self-awareness comes the realisation that their earlier creative work such as paintings and drawings do not actually look as much like their subjects as they originally thought. Alongside this growing awareness, the individual develops a shyness and perhaps embarrassment about their work that almost inevitably leads to inhibition. They stop painting freely, maybe they give up altogether. The innocence is lost: it will never be regained.

In his essay Kleist responds to this loss with the optimism. He argues that there is a way back to this freethinking, and it comes through the wisdom gained in study, learning and experience.

In his preface, Pullman discusses that the progression from innocence to self-awareness and then wisdom is what *His Dark Materials* is all about, and that his indebtedness to Kleist exists because it was reading *On the Marionette Theatre* that set him thinking about this change in the first place.

With learning comes wisdom, but I think it's also important to at least try to retain some of the naivety of childhood. Probably the thing that most inhibits us in our creative thought is our logical self, the part of us that likes following processes, that needs controls and inhibitions. I know I need my logical self – without it, quite apart from anything else, I would never get anything finished. However, I also try to ensure I leave space for my more freethinking self, the part of me that can imagine and picture the things that I then go on to develop and make.

While in my heart I want to disagree with Kleist and Pullman, with their thoughts on how we can never return to the naivety of our childhood, and of how study and learning can lead to the wisdom that once again enables and also deepens our creative abilities, I cannot. I have never studied painting or writing in the way I have studied mathematics. I found my first mathematics degree hard. I think this was due in part to the dry, disengaged teaching style of many of my lecturers, partly that mathematical theory was rarely related to the real world and, no doubt, my own immaturity. In many ways I rebelled against my studies, finding a solace and freedom in climbing. However, I now know how they helped me when later I returned to work towards a master's degree and then a

PhD. Perhaps even more fundamental have been the ways all this learning and research has helped me do useful things in the workplace.

Instead, I come to writing and painting in an intuitive fashion, following a need I have to explore myself, my intellect and my drive. While a part of me feels I could improve in both if I took the time to study their principles and processes, another part of me is afraid of what that might lead to. I worry that such learning would lead to the loss of the naive intuition I value so much. Mind you, so much of my work is rough and ready. I would love to learn more of the ways I could smooth it, refine it into something I could be more proud of. And there you have it – a classic dilemma. I don't yet know what I will do.

One thing I do wonder about Kleist and Pullman is whether they ever felt the pull of the mountains, how by simply being surrounded by them can take you to a state of calmness and creativity similar to the naivety of children. At least that's what I have come to realise I feel. I am beginning to think that this state of mind underpins perhaps all the other aspects of creativity I have discussed in this book. Surrounded by towering peaks, I lose inhibition because they remind me how unimportant I am. This in turn helps me to be brave enough to think freely, to follow my instinct and not worry about who or what suggests I am either wrong or that I should be doing things differently. Of course I may be wrong, but I won't know until I try, even if I fail I will learn, such failures are one of the quickest and best ways to learn.

CHAPTER
TEN

Running into Switzerland over the Grand Col Ferret

The path on the ground that took Andrea and I towards the climb up to the Grand Col Ferret was well-trodden and smooth, a grey ribbon laid down along the mountainside. It descended gradually, dropping down into the valley towards a few buildings and a refuge at Arnuva. We initially ran in the shadow of the mountainside as we contoured, reaching bright sunlight just before we reached the valley floor at its roadhead. After this the road turned to a dirt track that climbed the steepening ground as far as the Elena Refugio, following which were two or three miles of rocky single track up to the col.

The Elena is set on a small plateau that breaks the climb up to the col from the roadhead. It faces down and across the valley, looking back towards the Aosta Valley and the Col de la Seigne, and over to the bright white of Mont Dolent and its glacier above it. We stopped for a little while behind the hut to have a breather and put on sun cream.

We had been running for about an hour, but my legs were not getting going. They felt tired and heavy. This was not surprising given the previous two days' exertions, but it meant that an already tough day would feel harder. Given that I'd done the TMB before, I knew it wasn't a walk in the park and I was expecting to feel tired. I also knew that as long as I could trot along, and keep putting one foot in front of the other at a steady pace, we would get to our day's end, and to the end of the TMB the following day. I kept telling myself this. Rather than think about the length of the day ahead, which was daunting given how I felt, I just kept putting one foot in front of the other and focused on the scenery.

The path had loads of hairpins which steadily gained us height. It's a 600m climb to the col from the Elena – the path rocky and steep. I saw tyre tracks from mountain bikes as I climbed – the direction we were going we would have been carrying bikes if we'd had them, the descent heading the other way must be superb.

When we reached the col, we were met by two donkeys carrying food and other kit in bags strapped to their backs. They were accompanying walking groups, who'd climbed up to the col from the other side. The col itself marked the border and so we crossed it into Switzerland. Each of the high cols of the TMB is different, but each shares the Alpine beauty. I remembered the Grand Col Ferret as one whose views were stunning. The light was similar both times I've crossed it. Its brightness was almost fierce, giving a real distinctness to shape and colour. Looking east across the valley to the peak of La Tsavre, I had remembered the strong shadows cast on this mountain the first time I had been there. They were there again – this time I took a photograph and looked forward to the time I would paint this scene. I did this a few weeks later and I was taken back to the moment, and am again and again when I look at the resulting painting.

In the moment when I ran off the Grand Col Ferret further into Switzerland, I wholly appreciated the scenery but my body did not appreciate what I was putting it through. Less than ten miles in and I was really tired. Andrea sensed this but pushed us on, keeping the pace higher than my body wanted. We needed to get to a food shop down in the valley – Andrea was worried they would be closed at lunchtime and it was a long descent down to the village of La Fouly. The path was smooth and the descent gentle – we could run fast down here. Despite the sun shining so brightly, it was cool at our altitude with perfect conditions for running. It was just a shame my body was moaning so much.

Looking back now, I really don't know why we'd thought the route from the Bonatti to the Col de la Forclaz would be less than twenty miles. Wishful thinking I suppose – it was actually closer to thirty-five. I had a sneaking suspicion that it was actually longer when I saw a waymarker for the TMB that gave the town of Champex as 22km away. That was longer than we'd thought – I did the mental conversion to miles (about thirteen) and then – obviously not wanting to accept that we had a longer way to go than I had hoped – fooled myself into thinking it was only thirteen kilometres (about eight miles). Funnily enough I could only do this for so long before I realised I was wrong. This, of course, not only meant we had thirteen miles to add to the ten or so miles we had already covered, but also the distance from Champex to the Col de la Forclaz. The realisation of the length of the day, and what this meant for my tired body sank in as I trotted along. I came to the conclusion that I might as well just get on with it.

The shops were not shut when we got to La Fouly. This is a small village and the only one with a shop en route until Champex. We had both more or less run out of daytime snacks. I'd picked up a couple of chocolate bars at the Bonatti but only had half of one left, so it was a timely stop. We had a quick coffee in a cafe above the shop and then pressed on. The next stretch followed the Ferret river down the valley to the small hamlet of Issert. From here we would leave the valley floor, climbing up through forest to pop out at the edge of Champex.

It was when we arrived in La Fouly that I fully recalled this section of the route and its actual length from when I had run it before. What I had remembered as a couple of miles down the valley was more like ten. I think this was because the first time I had run it I was nowhere near as tired. I also remembered it for what it was – easy going and picturesque with one particularly memorable section that followed a ridgeline downhill in a pine forest, the trees forming an avenue down the ridge.

Andrea kept pushing the pace. After Champex there is a choice of route on the TMB to the Col de la Forclaz. She really wanted to take the higher variant over the Fenêtre d'Arpette. From the col she described the view to the Mont Blanc massif over the Trient Glacier – it sounded wonderful and listening to her talk about it, I wanted to take that way too. The alternate (and lower) route to the col de la Forclaz climbed over the Bovine – a ridgeline that itself had a great view down into the Sion valley and its surrounding mountains – but not quite as spectacular as the Fenêtre d'Arpette sounded. The Bovine would be the quicker route and would have been our choice if it was getting late in the day. Anyway, the decision made, Andrea kept us jogging along at a speed that wasn't really very fast but fast enough to make my legs grumble some more.

After a few miles the trail left the river and we climbed up the hillside for a little while towards the sweet-smelling Alpine pine forest. It wasn't long until we reached the avenue of trees. The path took us along this avenue, then downhill and back towards the river along a narrow ridge for about a kilometre. I remembered it from the first time I had run the TMB because it was unusual, different from the way terrain formed by a river normally lies. I had found it quite fascinating and beautiful. Looking at the map of the route, this ridge lies just before the junction of two rivers. The ridge must have been formed by these rivers over the millennia, each one gouging out land on either side.

We ran off the tip of the ridge back down to meet the river and crossed a bridge to reach a small village – Praz-de-Fort. Here we were at the opening of the Le Portalet valley, the clarity of the scene up this valley was wonderful – the sky a blue that offset the deep green of the trees, the lighter green of alpine meadow, grey rock and occasional snow patches higher up the mountainsides. At the time I had been inwardly focusing on my fatigue, silently grumbling to myself. Looking up Le Portalet reminded me why I had come, that the mountains of the Mont Blanc massif are special, and that I don't get to see them very often. That was enough to change my mood.

Le Portalet

They were making hay in the fields around Issert that afternoon. The heat bore down on us, it felt hazy, sleep inducing. In other circumstances I'd have welcomed the opportunity to stop under a tree and have a doze for an hour or so. Not today!

A few of the houses in the village are built into and around some large glacial boulders. Unique in their architecture, they reminded me of the Whillans Hut at the Roaches in Staffordshire or an old shooting hut up on Masham Moor in North Yorkshire, and also Moûtiers, a famous old village close to the Gorges du Verdon in Haute Provence. Each of these places is quite different from the others, but similar in idea – building into and around large boulders or a crag to form dwellings. Sometimes it's funny where association takes your mind. I love the combination of natural rock and human architecture, the making of something with great comfort and utility from solid, rugged objects with no immediate function for humans.

After Issert we crossed the main road as the route of the TMB leaves the Ferret valley. The climb up to Champex started, through fields at first then back into the pine trees. As we reached the forest beyond the meadow, the route climbed steadily through the trees. The valley we were leaving was wider here – it opens up to meet the expanse of the Rhone valley. The scenery in this part of the TMB contrasts with the parts closer to Mont Blanc. While we were, of course, not all that far away from that big mountain, we were on the very edge of the massif. To the north and east the mountains looked different – less glacial and greener, more people and roads.

The climb through the forest passed pretty quickly. We popped out of the trees on the edge of Champex and were soon standing next to the lake. In the Valais region of Switzerland, this town sits at a height of 1,470m. It is very picturesque, situated around the Lac de Champex. Since Victorian times it has been both famous and popular as a resort on the Grand European Tour. Today Champex is still popular as a holiday destination, and no wonder. High in the Swiss Alps, the comforts of a town and the lake while you're surrounded by pine forests and mountains. The town strikes me as somewhere requiring politeness and decorum. Given that it lies on the route of the TMB it goes without saying that they will be used to burdened, sweaty and grimy walkers and runners. Economically the town must welcome visitors like Andrea and me, but I got the feeling we would be out of place in many other ways – at least until we'd had a shower and change of clothes.

Like Courmayeur, Champex is a place I have only passed through, and one where it would be great to stay longer and explore a little of its history, have a swim or two in the lake, and just generally relax. Maybe I'm getting old. These days I seem to have more curiosity for the history of a place than I used to. I think part of that is because I find inspiration in the stories of adventurers past, in those who before me have themselves been inspired by the place. While Chamonix and Courmayeur share a history of Alpinism, Champex feels different. I don't know whether this difference reflects the fact that it is in Switzerland or because of its own particular history – perhaps both. Either way, I wouldn't have minded stopping a while to learn more of the place.

As it was we stopped just briefly to get an ice cream and another snack or two at a supermarket. I found some curry-flavoured cashew nuts which tasted divine – a sure sign that I needed to eat some salt and fat. Ice cream and strongly flavoured savoury nuts might seem a strange combination, but for me they were perfect. After this culinary delight we pressed on to the Col de la Forclaz. We had one more big climb to go and had yet to decide whether this climb would be the Fenêtre d'Arpette or the Bovine.

On leaving Champex the TMB follows the road out of town that heads north-west. The road signs showed it was not far to Martigny. I've travelled through this town a number of times when getting the train from Geneva Airport to Chamonix. From the airport the train travels along the south side of Lake Geneva, with tantalising views to the Chablis Alps across the water, passing through Lausanne and Montreux. On reaching Martigny I would change trains, taking the small but powerful Mont Blanc Express up the Trient valley and through a few tunnels to emerge at the head of the Chamonix valley. These days the increased number of shuttle bus services between Geneva Airport and Chamonix make this train journey largely redundant for me, from a practical perspective at least. While it's cheaper and quicker to get a shuttle, I always enjoyed getting that train.

By the lake in Champex

CHAPTER
ELEVEN

Switzerland is historically a place where people came for rest and recuperation. In a time when medics believed that mountain air was the best treatment for lung diseases, Swiss sanatoriums were popular with those who required treatment for such ailments and who could also afford to receive it high in the mountains. This was on my mind because of where we were and because of a book of Katherine Mansfield's I had recently read: *The Montana Stories*. The book is a collection of the short stories Mansfield wrote in her early thirties, while staying in a sanatorium close to the Swiss town of Montana in 1921, at a time she knew she was dying of tuberculosis. Champex and Montana are both in the Swiss region of Valais; as Andrea and I continued on the TMB we were not too far from where Mansfield stayed.

The book is the outcome of an extraordinary period of creativity in Mansfield's life. Despite being in pain and suffering she wrote and wrote, sitting at a desk in front of a large window with views of the mountains. Some of the stories in the book do not have an ending. Published unfinished, their reading is a poignant reminder of the limited time we all have. It must have been an incredible, desperate time for Mansfield, the intensity of living when you know your time is short. Bursts of creativity like Mansfield's can happen to those who know they are dying. Last year I heard a poem on the radio being read by its author, the Australian polymath Clive James. Dying of leukaemia, James was experiencing vividly the everyday sights and sounds he previously took for granted, appreciating their beauty and wonder in the knowledge that he would not be seeing them for much longer. His poem describes the wonder to be found in rainfall, and in a Japanese maple he can see in his back garden. He so much wants to live until the autumn when he will be able to see the tree in all its wonderful colours. The poem is beautiful, sad and yet so joyous. His appreciation for his garden, the tree and its wonder is enhanced by his knowledge that the autumn in which he sees it is likely to be his last. I found listening to him reading his poem moving and humbling, that a man could find it in himself to face death while still revelling in the wonders of living so creatively is both awesome and inspiring. In interviews I've heard and read where he discusses his poems, his trademark self-deprecating sense of humour shines through in joking about the fact that he is still around to talk about it in spite of his prognosis.

Listening to and reading some of the work of Clive James emphasised to me the beauty of the everyday and the value of memories. This is something I am beginning to appreciate more as I watch myself and my family grow older, and as Alanna has grown from a baby into a child.

There are times I want to ensure I savour and remember special things I want to hold on to. At the same time they remind me of experiences I have missed myself.

My dad loved to go walking, although I have mixed memories of mountains and moorlands from my childhood. When I was young 'the moor' was beautiful, but it was also bleak and desolate – somewhere you could get lost easily. Likewise, mountains were big, intimidating, at times fearful places. I think much of this fear stemmed from my dad's fretfulness about how dangerous they could be. He did venture out into them – rightly very proud of walking the Pennine Way when he was twenty – but he was always vocal about his fears of 'getting lost in the mist'. He passed these fears to me. Over the years I have overcome them by getting lost in mist many times, eventually finding myself, learning some more about map reading and navigation along the way. Mountains can be dangerous places but, as long as you have the right experience and equipment, the default attitude towards them should not be one of intimidation. It took me years to realise that.

The funny thing is that my dad loved high, remote places. He'd reel off the names of his favourite hills and the times he had on them – Cader Idris in Snowdonia, Stac Pollaidh in the north-west Scottish Highlands, Dartmoor's Yes Tor. When I was younger he used to try to get me, my sister and my brother to go hillwalking. We hated it, moaning all the way, which must have really spoiled his day. Thinking back now I really don't know why I did that.

Whatever the reason, it's a shame as I so wish I had walked with him more. I remember an evening stroll on the North York Moors. I must have been about seven; it was just me and him. We went a few miles, taking in the sunset after what had been a hot summer's day. For a change I did not grumble. On the way back to where we were staying we stopped at a pub. I had lemonade and some crisps, him a beer. He was very happy and I was too. I cherish that walk and the memory. These days I know how great it would have been to have had a few more.

Thinking of Mansfield, of James and my dad, reminds me of some of the things I take for granted in my life – my health and my relative youth. Hopefully I have decades stretching out ahead of me. Busy lives become full of hustle though. Fast movement and fast thinking from one thing to the next, not stopping to appreciate the simple things, the beauty in the everyday and the fact that I will not be around forever to appreciate them and everything else in my life.

Coming to the mountains enables me to reflect, to rest my mind in that I get away from the everyday. By that I don't mean to imply that I do not think while I run, but that I think differently. Perhaps mountains affect me in a similar way to how they did Mansfield. Being in the mountains helps me to think creatively, maybe because there is more space (and of course the inspiration) for creative thinking. Combine this with the almost robotic movement of putting one foot in front of the other as I run for miles kind of trips a switch in my head... surrounded by such space and shape I begin to unwind and to let my mind wander. I become less encumbered by the immediate challenges of day-to-day living. I think fancifully, ambitiously and – perhaps more than anything – in such a varied way. One moment I could be thinking about maths, another time about painting the scene I gaze on, then maybe even combining the two.

As we left Champex we had a route choice – the Fenêtre d'Arpette or the Bovine. The time of day and my general fatigue made the selection for us. The lower way, over the Bovine. I was disappointed and Andrea probably more so – she had climbed over the Fenêtre d'Arpette before and it had been a high point of the route for her. We contented ourselves with the fact that it would still be there the next time each of us had the opportunity to climb it. Mountains have a habit of doing that.

While the scenery and sense of place of the Col de la Fenêtre sounded awesome, it would be unfair to the Bovine to knock it too much. Not really a col, more the high point of a ridge that needed to be crossed to get to the Col de la Forclaz, the climb up to the Bovine is one I remember as being tough. The first time I did the TMB it was hot and I was tired, towards the end of a long day. This conspired with my lack of attention to the detail of the map to make it feel really tough. It was with a sense of trepidation that I was returning to climb the Bovine, given I had similar if not worse levels of fatigue.

The TMB route over the Bovine first passes by fields and a few chalets. After passing an enticing cafe the road turns to dirt, the route gently climbs through forest up the Jure valley. On reaching the head of this valley we would climb steeply out to the ridge of the Bovine and then descend off it to the Col de la Forclaz.

We passed the cafe. Quite soon from the track on which we climbed from the valley we could see the ridge we were heading for, high up on the hillside to our right. My memories of this as a tough climb were perhaps a good thing, better than the other way around, as it meant that I had mentally prepared for it. From the valley head we found a new path had been cut through the trees, making the going easier than I remembered. As we climbed up the steepest part I ate some sweets and gladly felt the sugar kick in a while later.

While I have been describing the Bovine as a second choice for our route, it has its own beauty. Sitting up above the treeline, the wide Rhone valley opens out below it. Here the TMB turns a corner around its north-eastern point. Our contour line over the Bovine passed some 1,500m above Martigny, a town on the valley floor. Martigny forms a juncture in the south-west corner of Switzerland. From it you can head south-east, over the Grand Saint Bernard Pass into Italy, or climb the Trient valley over the Col de la Forclaz and Col de Montets into France. Heading north-east up the Rhone valley takes you to through Sion and beyond, towards the town of Oberwald and the Rhone Glacier in the mountains above it.

I am most familiar with this area and its mountains from cycling trips I've had over the years. The high trails in the Swiss Valais region are superb to ride on a mountain bike and the road cycling Tour du Mont Blanc passes around here. This 210-mile cycle tour is double the length of the walker's TMB. It takes in a wider circuit of the massif and, in the Courmet de Roselend, the Petit Saint Bernard and Grand Saint Bernard passes, climbing a few of the finest road cols in the Alps. We were close to the route as we had run along the Ferret valley from La Fouly to Issert as it is just over in the next valley to the east.

As I climbed the Bovine, looking out to the Rhone valley, remembering my previous adventures here, the feelings I had during those times came flooding back. The day when I cycled from the Auberge de la Nova back in the Vallee des Glaciers, through Bourg-Saint-Maurice, climbing the Petit-Saint-Bernard Pass to Aosta, over the Grand Saint Bernard Pass and then, finally, late in the day arriving sunburned and tired at the Col de la Forclaz.

What a day's cycling that was and what thoughts ran through my head as I rode. The sheer size and spectacle of the Grand Saint Bernard Pass was incredible. A stunning place. I felt tiny as I cycled, following the hairpins and gazing all around as I as climbed to the high point, past the monastery at the col and then down, down, down for miles and miles from Italy into Switzerland, eventually reaching the valley and Martigny.

Fatigue passes... sometimes, to get beyond it, all you have to do is keep going. I knew that as I cycled the roads of the TMB that day and I knew that as I climbed the Bovine. The memories of these wonderful times stay with me. They give me strength. When I recall them in the future all I won't remember the weariness and the hunger, just the beauty.

When we reached the treeline the path became less steep. Fittingly there were cows close to the top of the Bovine, their bells clanging in proper alpine style. There was a little cafe that was shut, its ice cream flags hung down in the still of the early evening. We pressed on – not far now and all downhill after a last small climb to the highest point. I squeezed down another of my emergency energy gels and carried on.

Soon after we crossed over the ridgeline and back into the trees. With the valley dropping steeply to our right, occasionally we caught glimpses of the Col de la Forclaz and its hotel further ahead. Over the next half hour or so, Andrea commented that we did not seem to be getting much closer. It was about four miles down to the col; the trail through the woods was lovely, the evening light beautiful. By now my legs were very keen to stop. I felt really tired, more so than I had done for a fair few years. We ran through a little glade, the trail was rocky and I remember feeling very cross about that – why could the path not stay nice and smooth to make it easier going?

Finally we reached the road. Linking the Chamonix valley to Martigny and beyond, it is relatively busy. We crossed over, went to the hotel entrance, I took my shoes off, we went to check in. Stopping for the day at last. Running in one of my favourite places it might seem perverse that I had been wanting it to end for hours, but there you go. For some daft reason (wishful thinking?) Andrea and I had both thought we were in for a short day. It had turned out to be the longest of the trip – twelve miles and more than three hours longer than we originally thought it would be. While this is another lesson telling me I should pay more attention to the map when planning my day, I'm not sure I'll learn from this given I've been doing this kind of blasé planning for years. Every so often I end up ruing my laxness. To be honest, though, I kind of like it like that – it keeps me on my toes.

The Col de la Forclaz hotel has what looks to be some pretty classy hotel rooms and restaurant as well as a few *dortoirs*. A real contrast – one part of it there for well-heeled guests to relax at their leisure in their finery among finery. The other is there to serve other people, who may themselves be equally affluent, but this is hidden beneath their appearance – grimy, sweaty, perhaps limping, weary and most likely very happy.

We checked in and found our beds in an upstairs corner of the hotel. It was small – room for ten people – I picked one of the top bunks, got my least smelly clothes out of my rucksack and went to grab a welcome shower.
We were not too late to have missed the set dinner, but we'd already decided to eat from the bar menu that night. As a vegetarian who doesn't like cheese, is allergic to nuts and who isn't particularly fond of eggs, Andrea had gotten fed up of only being able to eat small amounts of what was on offer and I really fancied some chips. I would also have a beer or two. Given my physical condition I knew it would have been far better for me to stick to electrolyte drinks (and I did drink these too), but, frankly, the sun was still out, the view from the hotel garden was stunning, and we both just wanted to sit outside, have a beer and eat our dinner, soaking up the last of the day and our last evening of the TMB.

Unusually Andrea had a beer, the place and moment tempting her into it. We sat drinking lager and eating salted crisps, gazing up to the Col de Balme, the first climb of tomorrow and our gateway into France and the Chamonix valley. The burger and chips I ate that evening was probably the most expensive I have ever had, but also the most delicious; food is enhanced when you have been craving it all day and have a hunger driven by long days in the mountains. During the night, full of food, beer and tiredness, I would sleep on my back and snore my little heart out, once or twice even waking myself up with the noise.

The Col de Balme

CHAPTER TWELVE

Mathematics, rightly viewed, possesses not only truth, but supreme beauty. A beauty cold and austere, like that of sculpture, without appeal to any part of our weaker nature, without the gorgeous trappings of painting or music, yet sublimely pure, and capable of a stern perfection such as only the greatest art can show. The true spirit of delight, the exaltation, the sense of being more than Man, which is the touchstone of the highest excellence, is to be found in mathematics as surely as in poetry.

Bertrand Russell

The night was hot and stuffy, probably another factor which caused me to snore loudly for much of it. I'd not known I had snored quite so badly at first – Andrea told me afterwards, in the morning. Given my resentment of other snorers in shared dorms who keep me awake, I wished she had given me a few swift kicks or something. I felt rather apologetic, although none of our fellow sleepers seemed to be looking at me too resentfully as I collected together my kit and repacked my rucksack. We both did this quickly and soon were downstairs drinking coffee in the dining room. Breakfast was a croissant, bread, jam and orange juice. As I ate I realised I felt surprisingly good. After three days my body was tired and I really did think when we'd finished running the previous evening that I'd need longer than our twelve hours or so rest time to feel like getting going again. I started to think that maybe my body was beginning to get back into it, that I was regaining mountain fitness with each day.

We'd made an early start every morning, and were particularly keen to do so again that day to make sure we had a little time in Chamonix to have some food and sit in the central square, soaking up the view to Mont Blanc for the final time this trip. After breakfast, as I put my shoes on sitting on the steps of the hotel reception, the view was stunning. The mountains to the east carried a rosy pink light from the sunrise – alpenglow – I sat and gazed for a little while.

Given the location of the Col de la Forclaz, surrounded by steep mountains to the north and south, the warmth of the sun reaches it late in the morning and leaves early. It was cool as we started out, following the trail that took us down through the pine trees into the Trient valley. From here we would briefly follow the valley through the village of Le Peuty, before branching off to our right, where the route climbed a subsidiary valley up to the Col de Balme.

The smell of the pine forest was strong, the early morning still heavy with dew. This would be my last summer's morning in the Alps for a long time. I wanted it to last.

While the sun was not shining on us as we jogged through Le Peuty it was shining on the Trient Glacier, the snow gleaming in the morning light. Andrea had described to me the view over this glacier from the high point of the Fenêtre d'Arpette with great enthusiasm; she had wanted us to get there to see it again. While in a way disappointed that we had not got there, we both knew it would be there to be done another day. Sometimes one of the good things about leaving things undone is that you have a pull to go back to them.

From the Trient valley our first climb of the morning would take us to the Col de Balme. Over the years I have been here a number of times – the first time I ran the TMB, during runs out from Argentière in the Chamonix valley and a few times on a mountain bike. On the route of the TMB, it is another col that forms a national border, linking Switzerland to France, and is in a wonderful setting at the head of the hanging valley in which sits Chamonix and Argentière. You can see up to the col from the lower end of the valley at Les Houches. It is a small green saddle on a valley rim formed from towering mountains, ridges and crags – the highest line of least resistance over to the next stunning valley. If I was the col I would not much care for my political function – this comes and goes, and in a blink of an eye as far as any mountain range is concerned – but I would be proud of what I enabled, a high crossing point between two alpine valleys.

As the trail left the main valley we began climbing again, heading up through the pine to the treeline, meeting the sun as it began to warm the rock and meadow. We passed another party of walkers, sharing smiles and greetings on this beautiful morning.

The climbing felt easy. The path was gentle, forming shallow hairpins as it climbed up towards the col. Behind me and to my left I could see the mountains we had contoured the day before. The col itself was the only thing I could see ahead, but I knew what was coming. On cresting the pass the central massif stretched out before us, a shining white against the deep blue sky. The grass and flowers of the Alpine meadow blazed their green and yellow colours against the sky and mountains, and with the deep red of the Chalet de Balme's door and window frames. The col forms a terrace for the view to Mont Blanc. The highest mountain dominates the hanging Chamonix valley, its white ramparts always in view. The Aiguille Rouge, Aiguille du Midi and Aiguille Verte are just a few of the other mountains and rock faces that form the rest of the valley's skyline – one of the finest I will surely ever see.

I sat for a while on the soft grass and buttercups next to the Chalet de Balme, the little refuge that sits in the middle of the col. I enjoyed the moment, taking a few photographs. Here we were, back above the Chamonix valley having left it three days before on an all too brief but beautiful journey. We still had to descend to the Col des Montets, and then climb up the northern side of the valley towards the Index, Lac Blanc and La Flégère, along La Grand Balcon Sud.

My first time at the Col de Balme had been back in 2005. Aidan and I had spent a week in Chamonix with friends, before heading to Verbier and the Grand Raid Cristalp. I had ridden up to it from the Chamonix side on my mountain bike. Following a friend who was a mountain bike guide in the valley and knew all the trails, we took a route off the col which got steeper and steeper with more switchbacks and tree roots as we hit the pine forest. I came off my bike here, tumbling a long way down steep ground after falling – probably the closest I have ever got to completely losing it. Fortunately I managed to hold on to a tree root with one hand and my bike with another, scrabbling back up to the trail embarrassed and with a few scratches, happy to be in one piece.

From the Col de Balme the TMB heads to the Aiguille des Posettes, following the ridgeline towards the Col des Montets where the road reaches its high point on entering the Chamonix valley. We ran down the upper slopes of a ski run, the green meadow and buttercups nothing like the hillside's winter coat. The Aiguille des Posettes is a lovely runnable, ridgey hill, on reaching a small col between it and the Col de Balme we briefly climbed up to its summit.

The direct route off to the Col des Montets down the ridge of the mountain was initially steep and rocky, becoming a smoother path that levelled off in its descent about a third of the way down. By then it was mid-morning and getting hotter. There had been a light breeze at the Col de Balme which we lost as we got lower. The sun was very bright, making Mont Blanc dazzle as the sun reflected off its whiteness. The sky was a deep blue, the scene such strong colours – white, blue, the greens of the meadows and pine trees and the greys of the rock, crags and moraine.

In the pine trees we reached about halfway down to the Col des Montets it was cooler and more shaded, the contrast in light between this and the sunny mountainside significant. As we descended we passed two women on the path. They had stopped, looking into foliage on the side of the trail at a little brown snake. We stopped and watched it slither around the grass. It had bright black eyes and intricate diamond patterns. I can look at a snake's skin for ages; I find the myriad of colour and patterns enthralling. Nature made this, an original mosaic, mathematical and organic, yet another wonderful thing that has come from the wild.

The snake did not seem too bothered with us; it seemed pretty relaxed in the leaves and grass. Andrea and I were unlikely to have seen it had the two women not already stopped to watch it. Looking back I wonder what other wildlife we'd run past during those four days without noticing.

Running again after seeing the snake, we soon reached the Col de Montets and the road. On crossing the road we would immediately start climbing again, steeply up towards the Aiguille Rouge. Just set back from the road on its southern side are some boulders. We saw a few climbers bouldering, and a group who'd set up a top rope for some children to climb on one of the higher rocks. I've spent some time there, bouldering for the odd hour or so during some of my previous trips to Chamonix. It's an easy place to get to, a nice place to unwind by focusing on a few of the various problems.

Bouldering is low-level rock climbing in which the climber stays close to the ground so the risk of injury from a fall is minimised. This means that they can focus on pushing themselves – trying more difficult, powerful and technical climbing problems than they would if high off the ground with the risk of a roped fall. In my early twenties when rock climbing was my consuming activity in the outdoors, I got to a point where all I did was boulder. I do love it. Close to my home in Otley I am lucky to have some of the best gritstone bouldering at Caley, Almscliffe and the other crags of Wharfedale. I have spent many hours at these places, working boulder problems through, trying and trying to get a move and to link it up with others. Some people see it as lazy climbing, an easy way to gain the kudos associated with climbing without really having to work hard for it, reflective of our throwaway, consumerist society. While I can understand those views, it has always been more than that for me. The feeling of complete absorption – climbing at your hardest because you're only a few feet off the ground with minimal danger. This frees my mind and body to entirely focus on the series of moves required to get to the end of the problem.

I spent a few days in Banff in Canada in June 2010, waiting and making preparations for the start of the Tour Divide race. I had travelled light to Banff, only taking my bike and race-necessary kit; no space for books to read in the few days I spent there before the race. In a bookshop in downtown Banff I picked up a copy of Jon Krakauer's *Eiger Dreams*. A collection of Krakauer's essays published in journals and magazines, largely but not exclusively of a climbing nature, the second essay is entitled 'Gill' and tells the story of climber and mathematician John Gill.

Recognised by many as being the father of modern bouldering and, perhaps uniquely for a climber of this discipline, also recognised as being one of the most outstanding climbers of his generation. Early in his climbing career Gill turned his back on ropes and harnesses in favour of solving the pure and technical problems he encountered on rock boulders across wild and remote parts of the USA.

At first his contemporaries assumed he had lost his head – and his courage and daring. No longer climbing high cliffs, Gill was innovating and climbing problems of sheer intricate difficulty just feet from the ground. These problems seemed to lead nowhere, the satisfaction was wholly found in the climbing. Krakauer quotes comments from Yve Chouinard, a friend and climbing partner of Gill's: 'Gill had by then taken to eschewing summits, says Chouinard, and was "doing things for the sake of pure climbing, going nowhere".'

Krakauer writes how this has direct parallels to pure mathematics, of which Gill is a professor. Often with pure mathematics, an industrial application for a theorem is found years after the theorem is initially postulated or proven. Both bouldering and pure mathematics frequently have, therefore, no direct or immediate outcome apart from reaching the top of a small rock face or a stream of logic with a clear ending: closure. The satisfaction is found in the doing, in finding out what can be done and how it can be done.

That Gill is both a master boulderer and mathematician is no coincidence as he sees significant parallels between these two seemingly unrelated activities. 'When I first started climbing I met several other climbers who were research mathematicians,' Gill muses. 'I wondered, "Why is it that out of the few people I meet climbing, so many of them turn out to be research mathematicians?"

Even though one activity is almost completely cerebral and the other is mainly physical, there is something in bouldering that is akin to mathematical research. I think it has something to do with pattern recognition, a natural instinct to follow a pattern. What follows from this connection between pushing oneself physically and mentally in places of external beauty and in the internal beauty of logical and creative thought is enlightenment, which is amazing.

I was fascinated by this essay. It made a link between two seemingly disparate activities that resonated with me. It helped to understand why I find bouldering and mathematics so absorbing. Climbing a challenging boulder problem and innovating using mathematics are similar in that they require training and methodical thought, coupled with intuition and creativity. You can achieve something with one or the other of these but it is likely that the outcome will be lacking something – perhaps novelty, grace(fulness) or rigour.

> **For both ambitious boulderers and ambitious mathematicians, Gill emphasises, it's not enough merely to solve a particular problem: 'One of the objectives for both is to achieve an interesting result – ideally an unexpected result – in an elegant fashion, with a smooth flow, using some unexpected simplicity.'**

Experiencing the potential of innovation fuelled by methodical, rigorous thought and creativity is an exciting and stimulating place to be. Whether the outcome is a boulder problem, mathematical proof, statistical model or computer software, it is the same underlying process and, for me, leads to the same place.

This thinking leads me to consider whether, in my mind at least, the process of painting is similar to those I use to analyse data and design and develop software. All of these things require inspiration – a vision of what the finished product will look like or do. William Heaton Cooper alludes to this inspiration, and the analytical rigour required to take the inspiration and capture it as a painting, early in his book *Lakeland Portraits*.

> **If he is moved deeply by something he sees and wants to express, the artist must do a certain amount of conscious analysis, while at the same time pertaining to the emotional tension, or perhaps inspiration, that made him first want to paint it. Without this tension the final result will lack vigour and conviction. Without the analysis it will lack order, emphasis and unity.**

When I feel the urge to capture a scene in a painting or have an idea for some computer software in my mind, I don't immediately also see how I will do it. That is the problem that must be solved – the 'how' – and it is this part that I love the most. It can also be really frustrating to analyse and work through and sometime I fail, leading to spoiled artwork or a picture that just doesn't look like I'd hoped, a logical flaw or something I can't quite work out. I know, however, that this frustration and the failures associated with it are all part of the learning I seek. If every program worked first time and every painting turned out as I hoped, I would soon become bored and want to move on to something else.

The same was true for me with bouldering. I could spend hours, days trying the same problem, pushing myself to succeed, and to do it elegantly, with style. As we passed the climbers at the Col de Montet boulders I wondered if they were in that same place, relaxing in an almost meditative state between attempts on the few moves on a rock that so absorbs them.

On leaving the flat ground by the boulders the path began to climb steeply. I was very aware that this was my last climb of the TMB. In some ways I was glad of this, others not so – it was bittersweet. We pressed on up the rock steps, walking up into the south-eastern edge of the Aiguille Rouge, the mountains lying on the other side of the Chamonix valley from Mont Blanc. These peaks are rocky, spiky, tinged with a grey-pink that gives them their name. Their rock type is gneiss, and their colour comes from the iron contained within them. I have seen the Aiguille Rouge many times, probably the most memorable in the early hours of the morning when I was climbing the Mont Blanc du Tacul from the Vallee Blanche during my first visit to the Alps. As I stumbled up the mountain, light of breath from the altitude and roped together with my two friends Ellen and Sarah, we had turned to look behind us and saw an almost ethereal sight – sunrise behind the Aiguille Rouge. The mountains were monotone, offset against a fiery pink glow of the sunrise behind them. Breathtaking. That snow-plod up the Tacul had been my first alpine start. I realised then that this practice of making an early start – before sunrise – not only helps you climb the mountain safely, it gives you the opportunity to be awake and up high during one of the most beautiful times of the day.

Maybe seeing the snake on the other side of the valley had awakened my senses so I'd become more aware of the wildlife around us. Andrea climbed the trail ahead of me determinedly, not looking in the bushes at its side.

She didn't see the little brown deer chewing on some leaves, but I did. I stopped for a while, about two metres away from it, watching and taking photographs. In the bushes by the path the deer seemed very relaxed and not bothered about me being so close. After a few minutes I left it contentedly chewing leaves.

I didn't know what kind of deer it was, but I knew it wasn't an ibex and I'd been hoping to see one during this trip. I'd seen one once before, when I was with Aidan on the edge of the Vanoise National Park, an area of the French Alps in the Savoie region, to the south of Bourg-Saint-Maurice. Out walking on some high trails we passed an old hunter looking through the telescopic sight of his rifle. Friendly, he gestured for us to come and take a look. A beautiful ibex.

At the time I was filled with mixed feelings. I eat meat and this hunter was doing what he probably always had; hunting is a way of life for some in the mountains. But the ibex is such a beauty, it seemed a terrible thing to do. That particular ibex ran off down a scree slope and escaped. We continued up the path knowing that the guy was friendly and more than likely harmless – at least to us – but also knowing he had a rifle trained vaguely in our direction. I felt uncomfortable until we reached and crossed over the col we were heading for and completely out of his way.

The path began to level out as we reached a terrace on the mountainside. This was the Grand Balcon Sud – a high path that looks over to Mont Blanc and the Chamonix Aiguille that starts above the Col de Montets and finishes at Le Brévent at the western end of the hanging valley. Once you reach a height of around 2,000m, this trail contours the mountainside, running parallel to the Arve in the valley, undulating slightly from time to time. It is famous for its unsurpassed views of the mountains and we weren't disappointed as we ran along with Mont Blanc off to our left.

There were plenty of other people around. The Grand Balcon Sud is part of a network of trails on this side of the valley. They lead further into the Aiguille Rouge, to their highest summit the Aiguille de Belvedere and other landmarks such as Lac Blanc and Le Brévent. These trails are easily accessible from the valley, either under your own steam or by using one of the two cable cars from Chamonix up to Le Brévent or La Flégère.

We followed the trail until La Flégère cable car station, a point about halfway along the Grand Balcon Sud. And here I have an admission to make. We did not wholly complete the TMB. To do that we would have continued from La Flégère to Le Brévent, and then off the mountainside, back down to our start point at Les Houches. Instead we dropped down from La Flégère to Chamonix Le Praz and then strolled into town. Furthermore, we even took the cable car down into the valley.

A few years ago, not doing the whole of something like the TMB would have bothered me. I would have definitely run those last seven miles or so. However, it made sense to drop off the hill when we did – at least that's what I told myself. We were pressed for time and it was a choice between finishing the whole of the route and not being able to sit in the square in Chamonix, or heading down the mountain for some relaxing ice cream eating. In my head there was no contest.

We were quickly and smoothly back down in the valley. As we walked from the cable car station into Chamonix along the Arve river, Andrea and I agreed that a shower would be very nice. We each had at least eight hours of travel ahead – it would be good to do it smelling a bit less than we did, for our fellow passengers as well as ourselves. We were very happy to find that we could get one in the leisure centre on the edge of central Chamonix.

As I washed off the salt and grime it was with a real satisfaction at what we had done over the past few days. I was weary but it was that happy kind of weariness that comes with the finish of a long challenge. All things considered my body had stood up to it pretty well, my feet were still in one piece, and so was everything else. I was thirty-eight then – not old just yet but my body is beginning to tell me I'm no spring chicken anymore, I don't recover as quickly and as easily as I used to.

We left the leisure centre and ambled into central Chamonix where junk food gluttony began. I had a huge burger followed by a large ice cream. Andrea went straight for an even larger ice cream. I found the whistling and yodelling toy marmot I had been hoping to buy for Alanna in a souvenir shop and then we went for a coffee, sitting outside in the main square. Here I was again. I love this noisy, bustling, commercial place even though I shouldn't. Such a contrast to the mountains I love and yet a gateway to them, with so many lasting memories.

Sunrise behind the Aiguille Rouge

CHAPTER THIRTEEN

Much as I love the bustle of Chamonix, the quiet contrast of home is a strong draw – especially the Lake District. Buttermere is one of my favourite lakes in Lakeland, small and characterful, it nestles among giants. The water is a cool blue. It has a stillness that reflects its surroundings, the central and north-western fells. I particularly love swimming in lakes surrounded by mountains, and often take time to do this in the summer. The way a swim refreshes my body after a hard fell run is something hard to beat, and the tranquillity found in an early morning swim in beautiful fresh water with hills all around makes a very special place to be.

Since racing with Anna Frost and Chez at the MountainX race in the Alps I'd not seen much of Chez, but it's always good to catch up. Soon after the MountainX she picked up an injury which curtailed her running – something she has a talent for – and at the same time she started up a cycling business in the Lake District which has kept her and her partner Gavin busy. I see her occasionally when I'm there. We went for a morning swim in Buttermere back in the summer of 2010, a few days after I had returned home from the US after my failed attempt to cycle across it during the Tour Divide race.

Close to mid-summer and on a perfect morning, early and new, we pulled up in Chez's van. I followed her as she swam across the lake. In our wetsuits the chill of the water did not trouble us. Her glide in the water was more graceful, faster than mine. No matter, we were not racing, though how I would love to move more smoothly through this water, to feel less of an intruder in this other place. The world looks different from the surface of water. The familiar lines of the fells – Fleetwith Pike, Haystacks, Red Pike, Robinson – remain the same, but the way in which I look at them differs as from the land. My line of sight gently traverses the mountains as in turn I breathe alternately over my right and left shoulders. It all feels a lot calmer somehow.

I first started open-water swimming because I wanted to do the Helvellyn triathlon. To complete it I had to learn something new, and if I were to win it I would have to learn how to minimise my losses on my far weakest discipline. A graceful swimmer can achieve a speed that looks almost effortless – in reality it is anything but. Long-distance swimming isn't about splashing more, or pulling and kicking harder. It's all about minimising the resistance of the water, rolling your body from side to side so you slide and reduce your energy expenditure, rather than thrashing about wildly and tiring very quickly. Graceful has never been my style; my general approach to learning any new activity was far more brute force and ignorance – if you push hard enough it will go. For more brash, less thoughtful activities this could work; I learned quickly that it was not so with swimming. I had to learn properly, and that meant going back to the drawing board, taking my stroke and style apart, and putting it back together again.

It took me a while to relearn. I'd been taught as a child but that did not extend far beyond doggie paddle. At times while training it felt like I was making no improvements which, combined with the monotony of seemingly endless lengths in the pool, frustrated me, but the satisfaction I experienced when I felt and saw progress itself made my efforts and the time I put into it worthwhile. Aside from how learning to swim has helped me when racing, the pleasure I now get from open-water swimming is worth more to me than the benefits I gained when competing in races, chasing their occasional, elusive trophy.

We went for that morning swim in Buttermere back in the summer of 2010, a few days after I had returned home from the US after my failed attempt to cycle across it during the Tour Divide race. Three years later, over a cup of tea and a chat, Chez said that both she and Gavin had noticed the place I was in – distant and thoughtful – and had figured that my trip to ride the Tour Divide had been eventful for me emotionally and mentally as well as physically.

Mind you, I don't race as much as I used to and so don't hammer myself like I did for years. That probably helps. Racing is an addictive thing. If you commit to it, it can become all-encompassing – at least during the period of the race. I think that is part of the attraction – switch off to everything else and focus on pushing yourself physically as hard as possible, for as long as it takes.

For an obsessive person like me it is hard to let myself do things by halves, if I race I can't stop myself from trying hard, even if I am as not as fit as I used to be. After the Tour Divide – one of my biggest racing failures – a friend described me as an all-or-nothing personality. I have come to realise how right he was. Take racing out of the mountains, however, and there's still something left – you have the time and space to become absorbed in them in a different way. For me this different way is at least as fulfilling as racing – I think over the past few years it has become more important to me.

I think Nan Shepherd must always have known about this different way as she alludes to it throughout *The Living Mountain*, her wonderful eulogy to the Cairngorms.

> To pit oneself against the mountain is necessary for every climber: to pit oneself merely against other players, and to make a race of it, is to reduce to the level of the game what is essentially an experience. Yet what a race-choice for these boys to choose! To know the hills, and their own bodies, well enough to dare the exploit is their real achievement.

She understood the desire those who race have to test themselves, but emphasised throughout her book what can be found in taking the time to properly see.

> How could we imagine flavour, or perfume, without the senses of taste and smell? They are completely unimaginable. There must be many exciting properties of matter that we cannot know because we have no way to know them. Yet, with what we have, what wealth! I add to it each time I go to the mountain – the eye sees what it didn't see before, or sees in a new way what it had already seen.

I feel like I have begun to approach somewhere close to where Shepherd was, hopefully in years to come I will get closer still. There is so much more to a mountain than trying to climb it fast.

Companionship has become more important to me too. Since I have known her Andrea has always been a great friend on the hill, something I hope will continue for years. A few years ago I didn't think twice about taking off by myself for a few days' adventuring, nowadays I would probably not do so quite so lightly. That's not because I am fearful of hurting myself in any way although this is always at the back of my mind, more so these days. I think I now appreciate being with other people more than I did, and also find I spend too much time dwelling in my thoughts when I am by myself. I burned myself during the Tour Divide by riding solo and thinking too much; I'm not quite sure if I am over that yet. To be honest I don't know if I ever will be, or even if I want to be over it. During that trip I reached a limit in myself, and I think reaching that limit was what I wanted to get to – subconsciously at least – and not the finish line of the race I was riding at the time. In reaching that limit and being literally thrown back from it was almost like a switch was flipped. I stopped relentlessly driving myself to get the physical best out of myself, instead encouraging myself to back off a bit, enjoy the scenery, have a look at a few other things.

Perhaps the most obvious outcome of this change in me is that I chilled out enough to become a mother. Moving my head on enabled me to get to a place where I was ready to have a baby. It also helped me to release more of my creative self, opening the parts of my mind that had been numbed for well over a decade. In pushing myself further to write and paint I have surprised, delighted and frustrated myself in equal measure. Over the years I have found that these tensions are an important part of almost everything I do. In my work, research and art it feels like I seek them out, although they are really just the emotions that come along if you keep trying new things.

If reaching that limit in America helped me to become a mother, it also helped me to reflect more about my father. I went a little crazy in Montana, lost my mind for a while. I got myself back. This experience helped me to learn that I can get close without completely tipping over the edge. This learning was important because the most creative places in my head are also the most obsessive. Beyond them lies madness. I don't want to go mad, but I do want to spend time in these creative places so I need to get close to it. My experience at the Tour Divide helped me to realise that just because I am so like my father in some of his traits and his behaviours, it doesn't mean I have to become like him.

Another thing it has further instilled in me is I am not over him yet. I know I probably never will be. While the impact of the unstable behaviours of a mentally ill parent on their children has not yet been well researched, you do not have to be a rocket scientist to appreciate that it is very likely to be damaging. The memories of the way I felt when, as a child, I saw insanity in his eyes still haunts me. This is not something I often dwell on. I think over the years I have blocked out the bad memories because they are upsetting and because in my teens I came to the conclusion that I needed to get on with my own life.

There are positives too. I think that these days I am finding a peace. Over the past five years or so my outlook has changed. Writing this book has helped me to explore this change as well as indulge my love for painting and writing.

One thing I certainly shared with my dad is a tendency towards obsession. Mountains, running, cycling, climbing, painting, writing, mathematics and computing. I can get obsessed with all these things. Obsession can be a bad thing but it can also lead to the best outcomes. I have honestly found that things get the most intense, and I am probably the most unstable mentally, when I become obsessed with only one thing. Along with my obsession – and the pleasure I find – in mathematical modelling and systems design, the pleasure I find in painting and writing is something I need. Complete absorption, using my brain in quite a different way to maths, in doing them all I find a balance.

And then of course we have the mountains. I have already written one book about them, and here is another, this time full of paintings of them. I don't think my obsession with them will ever wane. If anything it has seemed to grow – I value them even more now I find myself being wowed by their colour and light.

These days my mountains generally come in intense bursts. The occasional weekend away to Scotland or the Lake District or a trip like the TMB... I need these times. They soothe me – wash away all of my hassles – I relax. At the same time I miss what I have back home – my family. I think this is the main reason why I seem to need companionship now – by myself I spend most of my time thinking about and wanting to be with my family. There is a paradox here, I feel an urge to spend time in wild and remote places and yet when I am there feel a strong pull to go home.

And the memories. Long summer trips when I was at university, eking out the few francs we had, learning of the beauty and ruthlessness of Alpine climbing. Mountain biking the trails of the valley, barbecues in the evening with friends, cycling through town while riding the TMB, arriving by train on the Mont Blanc Express and others. So it's the memories that make this place special for me, along with the view and the knowledge that there will be more of these times to come.

The Tour du Mont Blanc is a classic mountain journey. It is accessible, one you can take as long as you like over, and one that traverses some of the world's most beautiful high ground. The journey seems to be more important to me than the race these days. I still need goals, things to strive for, but I am increasingly finding I don't need to try to beat other people– or myself – as I do so. I think the mountains will always inspire me to challenge and push myself. These days they also inspire me to reflect and think creatively, and for that I love them even more.

EPILOGUE

Lives close to me have come and gone since my run with Andrea. In 2016 I had my second baby girl and in the spring of 2017 my dad died. I was pleased he got to see his new granddaughter and was happy with my family before he went.

The year after his death was a dark time. It is the first time I have experienced such grief in its rawness. Dad's passing was not only tremendously sad, it dredged up memories I had left buried for years in hidden places in my mind. It took my dear friend Andrea to tell me that I could give these memories away, that I did not need to own them and they need have no hold over me. Now I realise that even if there will not be an end to this grief, with time it is becoming easier.

Some of the things I learned while writing this book now seem obvious, which to me shows the value of this kind of exploration. Over the past ten years I have grown to love the process of writing and painting. The journey towards the making of a book is just another kind of adventure, and one where you're never really sure about your destination until you arrive.

ACKNOWLEDGEMENTS

I have found writing a book takes a lot of stubbornness – something I have plenty of. Getting a book ready for publication takes other things too.

Constructive feedback helps, and encouragement means a lot. Thank you to Clare Carter for her feedback on this book's initial workings. Thank you also to Helen Mort, who read an early draft and gave me the encouragement to carry on.

High Inspiration wouldn't be here without Jo Allen and Rhiannon Hughes – two people whose editing, design skills and enthusiasm have made this book far more than it otherwise would have been. And thank you to John Houlihan for taking the time on a windy day for my author photograph.

Thank you to Aidan, Alanna and Robyn.

BIBLIOGRAPHY

Bonatti, Walter, *The Mountains of My Life*, Penguin Classics, (1995)

Cawthorne, Mike, *Wild Voices: Journeys Through Time in the Scottish Highlands*, Birlinn Ltd, (2014)

Cooper, William Heaton, *Lakeland Portraits*, Hodder & Stoughton, (1954)

Douglas, Ed, *A Muscular Imagination – Andy Parkin and the Art of Climbing*, Alpinist Issue 28, (2009)

Gunn, Neil, *The Well at the World's End*, Faber & Faber, (1951)

Gunn, Neil, *Highland River*, Canongate, (1937)

James, Clive, *Sentenced to Life*, Picador, (2015)

Kleist, Henrich, *Uber das Marionetten Theater*, Berliner Abendblatter, (1810)

Krakauer, Jon, Eiger Dreams, *Ventures Amoung Men and Mountains*, The Lyons Press, (1990)

MacDonald, Helen, *H is for Hawk*, Jonathan Cape, (2015)

Macfarlane, Robert, *Mountains of the Mind*, Granta Books, (2003)

Macfarlane, Robert Macfarlane, *The Wild Places*, Granta Books, (2007)

Mansfield, Katherine, *The Montana Stories*, Persephone Books Ltd, (2001)

Moffat, Gwen, *Space Below My Feet*, Hodder & Stoughton, (1961)

Norbury, Katharine, *The Fish Ladder*, Bloomsbury, (2015)

Pullman, Philip, *His Dark Materials*, Scholastic, (1995-2000)

Shepherd, Nan, *The Living Mountain*, Canongate, (1977)

Whittle, Jamie, *White River: A Journey Up and Down the River Findhorn*, Sandstone Press, (2003)

From *H Is For Hawk* by Helen Macdonald, published by Jonathan Cape. Reproduced by permission of The Random House Group Ltd.

Katharine Norbury, *The Fish Ladder*, Bloomsbury, London, 2015. Reproduced by kind permission of A P Watt at United Agents and Bloomsbury Publishing PLC on behalf of Katharine Norbury.